Ceramic Figures

A DIRECTORY
OF ARTISTS

MICHAEL FLYNN

A & C BLACK • LONDON

RUTGERS UNIVERSITY PRESS
NEW BRUNSWICK • NEW JERSEY

First published in Great Britain 2002
A & C Black Publishers Ltd
Alderman House
37 Soho Square
London W1D 3QZ
www.acblack.com

ISBN 0-7136-5117-2

Simultaneously published in the US by
Rutgers University Press
100 Joyce Kilmer Avenue
Piscataway, NJ 08854-8099

ISBN 0-8135-3205-1

Cover illustration (front): *Angel Flight*, 1988, raku fired
clay with concrete base, by Michael Flynn.
Cover illustration (back): *Devil Walk*, 1986, mixed
media, by Howard Kottler.
Frontispiece: *Catching the Cock*, by Michael Flynn.

Book design by Penny and Tony Mills
Cover design by Dorothy Moir

Printed and bound in Italy by G. Canale & C. S.p.A.

Introduction

The last 35 years has seen a burgeoning interest in fired clay as an expressive medium not necessarily related to the vessel. Within this movement there have been significant developments with regards to the human figure and sculptural ceramics.

This book sets out simply to present as wide a spectrum as possible of these developments world wide. It is very deliberately a book of images rather than text. I hope that the images will speak for themselves without my needing to describe, explain or otherwise comment on them. The biographies are also deliberately sparse because I want the images to stand independent of superfluous (even though it may be interesting) information.

Given that I am myself involved in this movement, I have tried hard to be objective in my selection of artists. I have included work which I do not necessarily like but which I feel has a legitimate place within the wider scheme of things. What may be seen as overly grotesque or naive to one national or social group, can be highly lauded by another.

There are thousands of people producing figurative ceramics, more in western societies than in eastern. Often I have had to select one person as representing a particular approach where several could have served as examples. In such cases I have tried to focus on those people who were the instigators of, or who seem to have achieved most within that approach.

With regards to where an artist's work can be seen, I have made a rather arbitrary selection given that there are many hundreds of collections and not enough space to include them all.

Acknowledgements

I would like to thank all the artists and galleries who have generously supplied images and information for the book, especially Garth, Mark and Gretchen at the Garth Clark Gallery.

KEY TO COUNTRY CODES

A	Austria	DK	Denmark	IRL	Ireland	PL	Poland
ARG	Argentina	E	Spain	ISR	Israel	RUS	Russia
AUS	Australia	EST	Estonia	JAP	Japan	TH	Thailand
B	Belgium	FIN	Finland	LT	Lithuania	TRK	Turkey
CAN	Canada	GB	Great Britain	LV	Latvia	TW	Taiwan
CH	Switzerland	GR	Greece	N	Norway		
CZ	Czechoslovakia	H	Hungary	NL	Netherlands		
D	Germany	I	Italy	NZ	New Zealand		

List of artists

AUSTRALIA
Fell, Fiona
Klix, Gudrun
Peascod, Alan
Srivilasa, Vipoo (TH)

AUSTRIA
Dietz, Gundi
Smolik, Gerda

ARGENTINA
Fontana, Lucio (I)

BELGIUM
Dionyse, Carmen
Hoys, Marnix
Muys, Hermann
Pauwels, Achiel
Vermeersch, José

CANADA
Payce, Greg
Williams, Gary

CZECH REPUBLIC
Paral, Miroslav
Purkrábková, Hana
Viková, Jindra

DENMARK
Hole, Nina

FINLAND
Mákelá, Maarit

FRANCE
Bignolais, Gérard
Capron, Roger
Corregan, Daphné (USA)
Fischer, Wayne (USA)
Jeanclos, Georges

GERMANY
Grzimek, Jana
Haug, Nica
Hebenstreit, Theresia
Fischer, Lothar
Möhwald, Gertraud
Neubert, Martin
Onnen, Sybille
Schmidt-Reuther, Gisela
Schultze, Klaus
Sturm, Robert

GREAT BRITAIN
Barrett-Danes, Alan
Barrett-Danes, Ruth
Barton, Glenys
Bennett, Tony
Brown, Christie
Brown, Sandy
Brownsword, Neil
Bryars, Jill
Crowley, Jill
Curneen, Clare (IRL)
Cushway, David
Dixon, Stephen
Eglin, Philip
Flynn, Michael (IRL)
Fuller, Geoffrey
Henry, Sean
Heyes, Tracey
Jones, Allen
Jupp, Mo
MacDonnell, Sally
Mitchell, Craig
Simon, Laurence (F)
Walker, George

GREECE
Karakitsos, Kostas
Kerassioti, Maro
Triantifillou, Lena

HUNGARY
Fekete, Laszlo
Fusz, Geörgy
Geszler, Maria
Kecskeméti, Sándor
Schrammel, Imre

IRELAND
Keeney, Christy

ISRAEL
Yatom, Varda

JAPAN
Tsutsumi, Nobuko

POLAND
Kalkowski, Kazimiera
Kuczynska, Maria Teresa
Zamorska, Anna-Malicka

LITHUANIA
Janusonis, Audrius
Kvastye, Jolante

NETHERLANDS
Struktuur 68
Freijmuth, Alphons
Lucebert
Snoek, Jan
Van Bentem, Hans
Weigman, Diet

NEW ZEALAND
Verdcourt, Ann

RUSSIA
Tsivin, Vladimir

SWITZERLAND
Glave, Patricia

USA
Arneson, Robert
Autio, Rudi
Bakst Wapner, Grace
Buonagurio, Tony
Burns, Mark
de Staebler, Stephen
Earl, Jack
Frank, Mary
Frey, Viola
Gonzalez, Arthur
Held, Marion
Isupov, Sergei
Jeck, Doug
Kottler, Howard
Lucero, Michael
Moonellis, Judy
Nadleman, Elie
Novak, Justin
Oka Doner, Michelle
Perrigo, Anne
Shimazu, Esther
Stern, Melissa
Takamori, Akio
Wood, Beatrice
Woodward, John
Youngblood, Daisy

Please note: artists have been listed under the country in which they now live and work, rather than their country of birth, if different.

Arneson, Robert

American. Born Benicia, California (USA), 1930.

Initiator of the Funk Movement. Played an extremely important role in establishing ceramic as a major sculptural medium. Teaching at the University of California in the 1960s, focusing on ideas and content rather than form and process. Work is to be found in most major collections throughout the world. Represented by George Adams Gallery, New York (see appendix 2). Died Benicia, California, 1992.

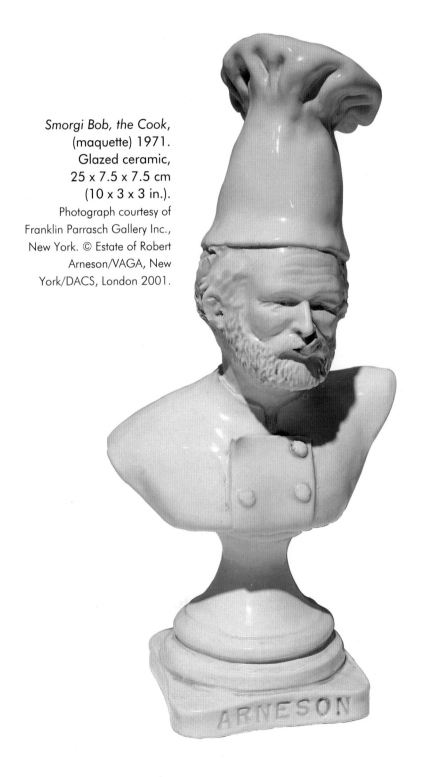

Smorgi Bob, the Cook, (maquette) 1971. Glazed ceramic, 25 x 7.5 x 7.5 cm (10 x 3 x 3 in.). Photograph courtesy of Franklin Parrasch Gallery Inc., New York. © Estate of Robert Arneson/VAGA, New York/DACS, London 2001.

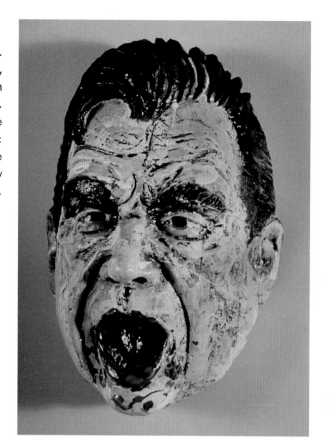

Raw Bacon, 1981.
Glazed ceramic,
13 x 25 x 15 cm
(5 ⅛ x 10 x 6 in.).
Photograph courtesy of George
Adams Gallery, New York. Collection:
John and Mary Pappajohn. © Estate
of Robert Arneson/VAGA, New
York/DACS, London 2001.

Guardians of the Secret II,
1990.
Glazed ceramic, metal, wood,
plexiglass, canvas and acrylic,
218 x 302 x 66 cm
(86 x 119 x 26 in.).
Photograph courtesy of George
Adams Gallery, New York.
© Estate of Robert Arneson/VAGA,
New York/DACS, London 2001.

His and Her Bricks, 1971.
Unglazed terracotta, approx.
11 x 25.5 x 7 cm (4 ¼ x 10 x 2 ¾ in.).
Photograph courtesy of Franklin Parrasch Gallery
Inc., New York. © Estate of Robert Arneson/VAGA,
New York/DACS, London 2001.

Scale, 1965.
Glazed earthenware,
11 x 37 x 32 cm
(4 ¼ x 14 ⅝ x 12 ½ in.).
Photograph courtesy of Franklin
Parrasch Gallery Inc., New York.
© Estate of Robert Arneson/VAGA,
New York/DACS, London 2001.

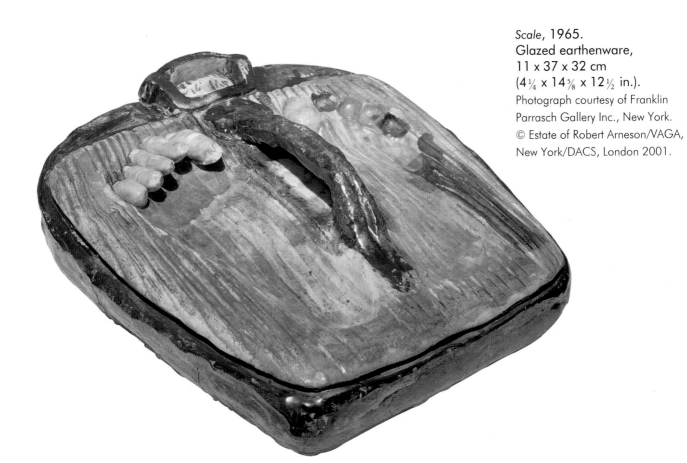

Autio, Rudi

American. Born Butte, Montana (USA), 1926.

A major figure in American ceramics and internationally for over 40 years. Has worked in a variety of media including bronze, glass and fabricated metal. He is best known for his figurative vessels which are to be found in museums and collections all over the world. Lives and works in Missoula, Montana (USA).

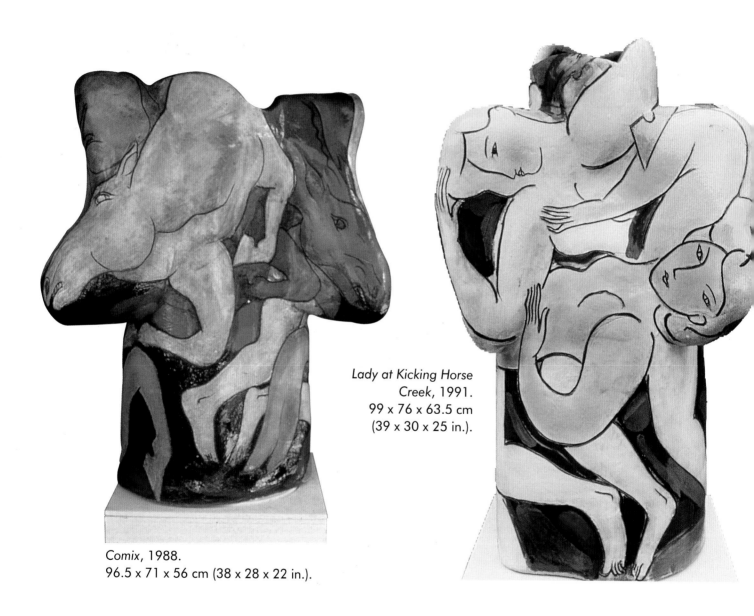

Lady at Kicking Horse Creek, 1991.
99 x 76 x 63.5 cm
(39 x 30 x 25 in.).

Comix, 1988.
96.5 x 71 x 56 cm (38 x 28 x 22 in.).

Metaphor, 1998.
75 x 73.5 x 54.5 cm
(29½ x 29 x 21½ in.).

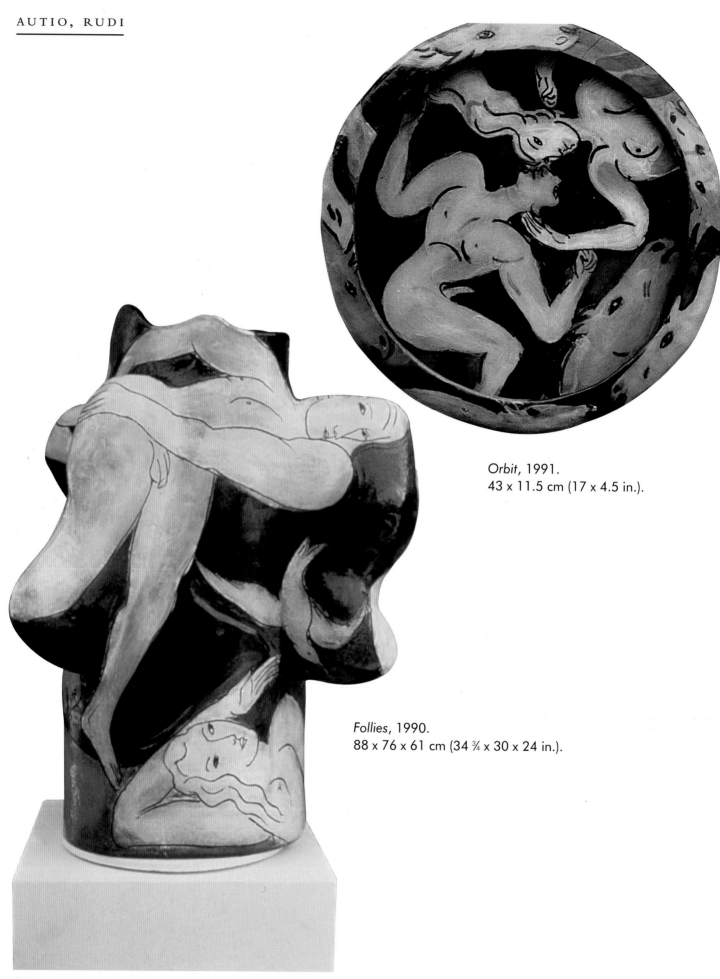

Orbit, 1991.
43 x 11.5 cm (17 x 4.5 in.).

Follies, 1990.
88 x 76 x 61 cm (34 ¾ x 30 x 24 in.).

Bakst Wapner, Grace

American. Born Brooklyn, New York City (USA), 1934.

Has shown widely in the United States. Collections include: Sol Lewitt Collection, New York (USA); the Gibbes Museum, Charleston, South Carolina (USA). Lives and works in New York City (USA).

The Kiss, 1994.
High-fired clay, 37 x 52 x 32 cm (14½ x 19½ x 12½ in.).
Photograph courtesy of Steinbaum Krauss Gallery, New York.

Self Portrait, 1993.
High-fired clay, pigment.
38 x 38 x 21.5 cm (15 x 15 x 8 ½ in.).

RIGHT
Ribcage, 1996. High-fired clay, pigment, 305 x 28 x 23 cm (120 x 11 x 9 in.).

FAR RIGHT
We Know the Inaccuracy of Radiocarbon Dating, 1998. High-fired clay, pigment, 43 x 23 x 33 cm (17 x 9 x 13 in.). Photograph courtesy of Steinbaum Krauss Gallery, New York.

RIGHT
And Hugged the Narrow Ledge, 1997. High-fired clay, pigment, 38 x 25 x 33 cm (15 x 10 x 13 in.). Photograph courtesy of Steinbaum Krauss Gallery, New York.

FAR RIGHT
Bone of My Bone, 1995. High-fired clay, pigment, 43 x 23 x 15 cm (17 x 9 x 6 in.).

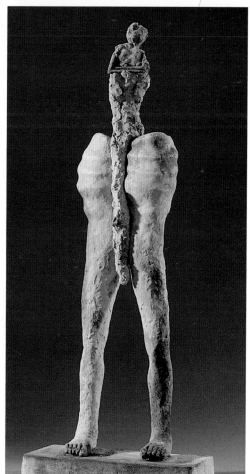

9

Barrett-Danes, Alan and Ruth

British. Alan born Gillingham, Kent (GB), 1935. Ruth born Portsmouth (GB), 1940.

Worked together in the 1970s developing joint concepts for which Ruth modelled the figures and Alan worked on any thrown elements and appropriate glazes, engobes etc. Later Alan returned to the vessel and Ruth continued to work figuratively *(see opposite)*. Collections include: the National Museum of Wales (GB) (see appendix 1); Melbourne Museum and Art Gallery (AUS). Work mostly in porcelain. Both live and work in Abergavenny, Gwent, Wales (GB).

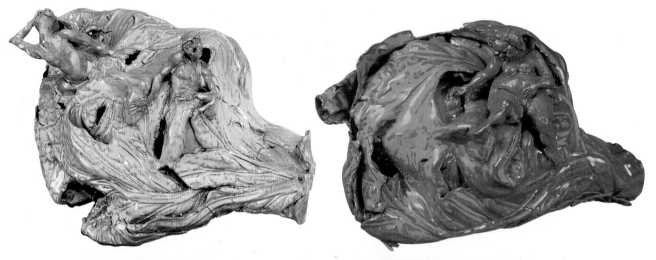

ABOVE, FAR LEFT
Alan & Ruth Barrett-Danes, *Cabbage Piece*, 1975.
Porcelain, height: 12 cm (4¾ in.).

ABOVE
Alan & Ruth Barrett-Danes, *Cabbage Piece*, 1976.
Porcelain, height: 14 cm (5½ in.).

LEFT
Alan & Ruth Barrett-Danes, *Chair Piece*, 1978.
Porcelain, height: 20 cm (8 in.).

Ruth Barrett-Danes, *Supporting The Party*, 1996.
Porcelain, height: 30 cm (11¾ in.).

Ruth Barrett-Danes, *Dancing Contest*, 1996.
Porcelain, height: 34 cm (13½ in.).

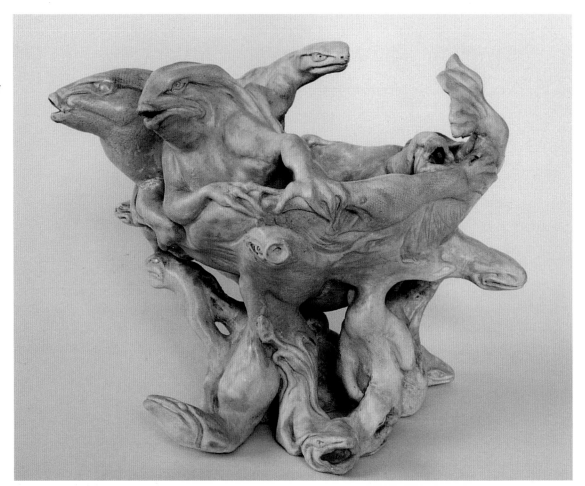

Ruth Barrett-Danes,
Fruits de Mer, 2000.
Porcelain, height:
26 cm (10 ¼ in.).

Barton, Glenys

British. Born Stoke-on-Trent (GB), 1935.

An important figure at the cutting edge of the new British ceramics in the early 1970s. She has always distanced herself from the craft/ceramic category, wishing to be judged purely in terms of sculpture. Represented by Flowers East, London (see appendix 2). Collections include: the National Portrait Gallery, London (GB); Boymans-Van Beuningen Museum, Rotterdam (NL) (see appendix 1). Lives and works in London (GB).

Profile Head II (Richard IV, Richard I, Pink Madonna), 1986–88.
Height: 66 cm (26 in.).
Photograph courtesy of Flowers East, London.

Jacqui and Richard,
1985–6.
41 x 38 cm
(16 x 15 in.).
Photograph courtesy of
Flowers East, London.

Amanda I, 1995.
56 x 41 x 15 cm
(22 x 16 x 6 in.).
Photograph courtesy of
Flowers East, London.

Time at Yagul, 1976–77.
Bone china, height: 17.5 cm (7 in.).
Photograph courtesy of Flowers East, London.

Bennett, Tony

British. Born Evesham, Worcestershire (GB), 1949.

Since 1975, lecturer in Ceramics at Hastings College of Art and Technology. Shows regularly in Britain and in Garth Clark Gallery, New York (see appendix 2). Collections include: Auckland Museum (NZ); Shigaraki Ceramic Cultural Park (JAP) (see appendix 1). Mostly slipcast or press-moulded, sprayed earthenware. Lives and works in St Leonards on Sea and Hastings, Sussex (GB).

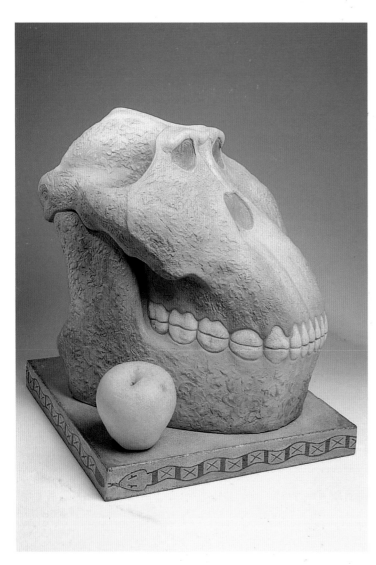

BELOW
Red Devil Teapot, 1993.
Slipcast earthenware with coloured slips, earthenware glazes and onglaze enamels, height: 50 cm (19 ¾ in.).

ABOVE
Adam, 1993.
Press-moulded head, slab-built base, moulded apple, hand painted and sprayed earthenware glazes, height: 36 cm (14 ¼ in.).

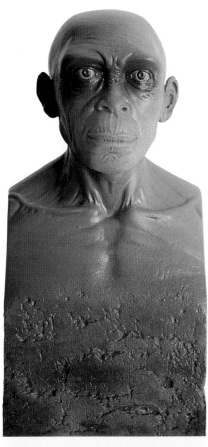

FAR LEFT
Neanderthal, 1979.
Slipcast earthenware with
sprayed earthenware glaze,
height: 30 cm (11¾ in.).

LEFT
Riot Cop, 1972.
Slipcast earthenware, hand painted
underglazed sprayed with earthenware
glaze, height: 51 cm (20 in.).

BELOW LEFT
Urban Camouflage, 1997.
Press-moulded, slipcast, handpainted,
earthenware glaze, height:
41 cm (16 in.).

BELOW
Ghost Dance, 1997.
Coloured earthenware slips painted
into mould, fired once and burnished,
height: 59 cm (23¼ in.).

Bignolais, Gérard

French. Born Bourges (F), 1937.

Has been exhibiting prolifically since 1971, mostly in Paris. Collections: the National Gallery, Prague (CZ); Fond Departmental d´Art Contemporain de Seine Saint-Denis (F). Figures press-moulded from body casts, usually salt-fired. Lives and works in Antony (F).

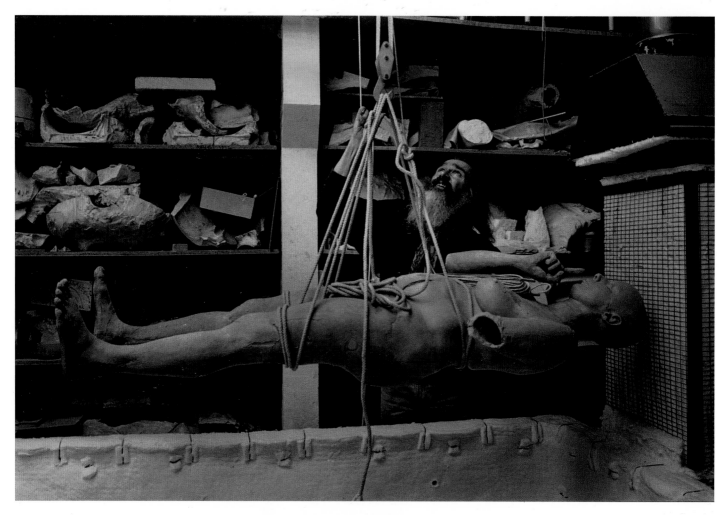

Bignolais In Studio, 1997.
Press-moulded and salt-fired,
height: approx. life-size, 150 cm (59 in.).
Photograph by Sabine Weiss.

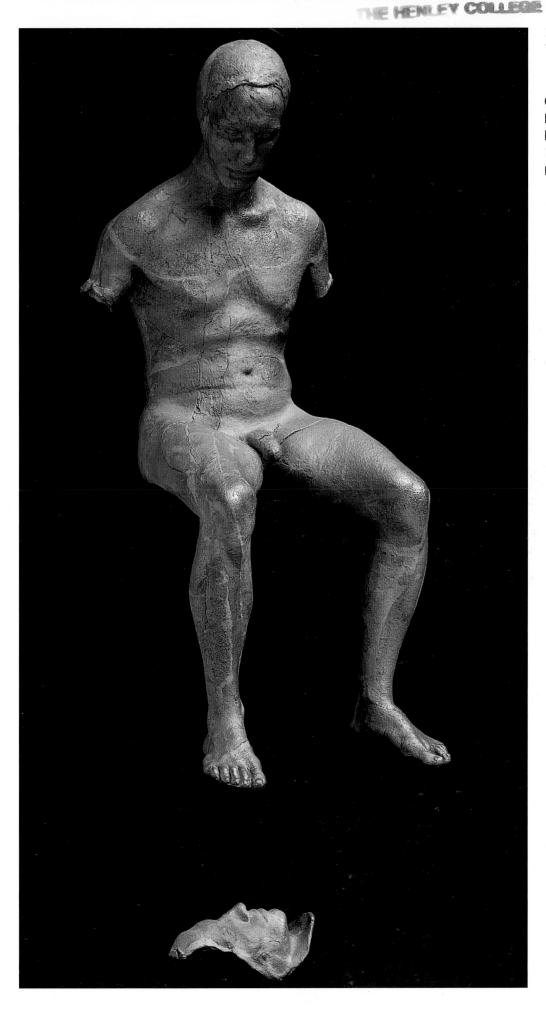

Guetteur, 1995.
Press-moulded and salt-fired,
height: approx. life-size,
150 cm (59 in.).
Photograph by Pascal Bignolais.

ABOVE
Anne et Dominique, 1997.
Press-moulded and salt-fired,
height: 160 and 155 cm
(63 and 61 in.).

BELOW
Groupe, 1997.
Press-moulded and salt-fired,
height: approx. life-size, 150–60 cm (59–63 in.).

Brown, Christie

British. Born Yorkshire (GB), 1946.

Since 1993 lecturer in Ceramics, at the University of Westminster, London (GB). A well-known and highly active figure on the British ceramic scene. Collections include: Victoria and Albert Museum, London (GB); the Musée National de Ceramique, Sèvres (F) (see appendix 1). Lives and works in London (GB).

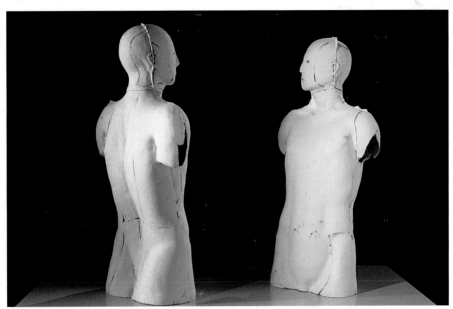

The Delphic Twins, 1996.
73 x 34 x 21 cm (28 ¾ x 13 ½ x 8 ¼ in.).
Photograph by David Rowan.

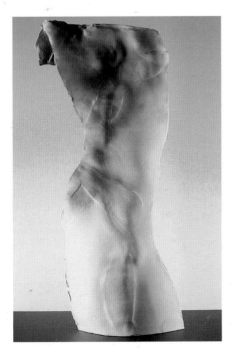

White Male Figure, 1988.
Height: 82 cm (32 ½ in.).
Photograph by Tim Imrie.

Lynette Reclining, 1990.
74 x 64 x 13 cm
(29 ¼ x 25 ¼ x 5 in.).

RIGHT
Red Olympia, 1999.
Brick clay,
171 x 43 x 36 cm
(67 ½ x 17 x 14 ¼ in.).
Photographed in the
Wapping Hydraulic Power
Station, from the exhibition
Fragments of Narrative,
commissioned by WPT.
Photograph by Kate Forrest.

FAR RIGHT
Stone Mother, 1995.
78 x 31 x 18 cm
(30 ¾ x 12 ¼ x 7 in.).
Photograph by
David Rowan.

BELOW
*Curious Automaton,
Stonemother 4* and
Delphic Twins.
(Group shot of three
installations at Kingsgate
Gallery, London, 1996).

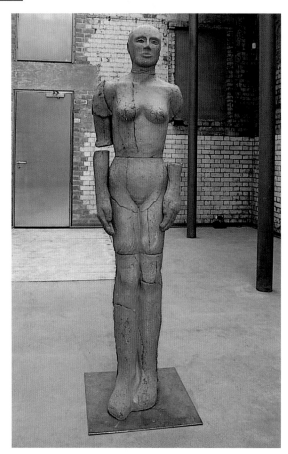

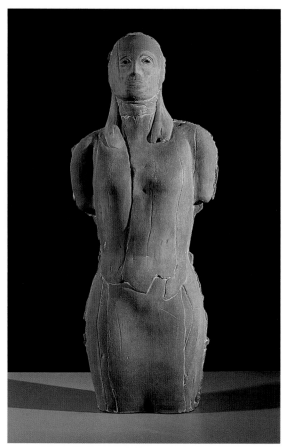

Brown, Sandy

British. Born Tichborn, Hampshire (GB), 1945.

Ceramic career began in Japan in 1969. Makes a large range of pots, ceramic wall pictures, paintings and drawings as well as her female/goddess figures which are very well-known in Britain and in Germany. Collections include: the Victoria and Albert Museum, London (GB) (see appendix 1); the Winnepeg Museum of Art, Canada. Lives and works in Bideford, Devon (GB).

ABOVE
Cheeky Figure, 1988.
Glazed stoneware,
height: 60 cm (23 ¾ in.).
Photograph by Takeshi Yasuda.

ABOVE, RIGHT
Full Moon Goddess, 1990.
Stoneware, height: 180 cm (71 in.).
Photograph by Takeshi Yasuda.

RIGHT
Earth God and Earth Goddess, 1994.
Unglazed stoneware,
45.5 x 43 cm (18 x 17 in.).
Photograph by John Andov.

*Goddess with Serpent
and Angels*, 1992.
Stoneware, height:
65 cm (25 ½ in.).
Photograph by Stephen Brayne.

Female Figure, 1998.
Smoked earthenware, height: 35 cm (13 ¾ in.).
Photograph by John Andov.

Brownsword, Neil

British. Born Stoke-on-Trent, Staffordshire (GB), 1970.

Exhibiting regularly, mostly in Britain, since leaving the Royal College of Art, London (GB) in 1995. Collections include: the Crafts Council of Great Britain, London (GB) (see appendix 1); Manchester University Study Collection (GB). Lives and works in Stoke-on-Trent (GB).

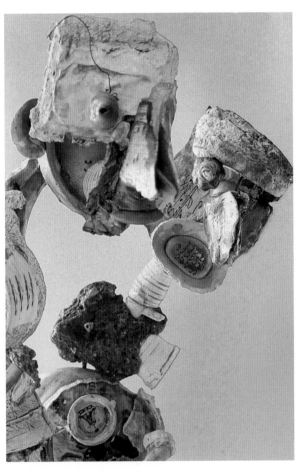

She Wants Your Junk, (detail) 1998. Ceramic collage, metal, found objects, height: 42 cm (16 ½ in.).

Loose Lips Sink Ships, (detail) 1997. Ceramic collage, height: 24 cm (9½ in.).

Feel So Down 'Cause You Haven't Made Out, 1999.
Ceramic collage, metal, found objects, height: 37 cm (14 ½ in.).

Wishing I Was Pretty, (detail) 1999.
Ceramic collage, metal, found objects, height: 40 cm (15 ½ in.).

Not Tonight, 1995.
Ceramic collage, height: 85 cm (33 ½ in.).

Bryars, Jill

British. Born Midhurst, West Sussex (GB), 1966.

Working in own studio in Petersfield (GB) since completing MA Ceramics at Cardiff (South Glamorgan Institute of Higher Education) in 1997. Lives in Whithall, Hampshire (GB).

Crouching Bird Figure, 1998.
Height: 40 cm (15 ¾ in.).
Photograph by Nigel Collins.

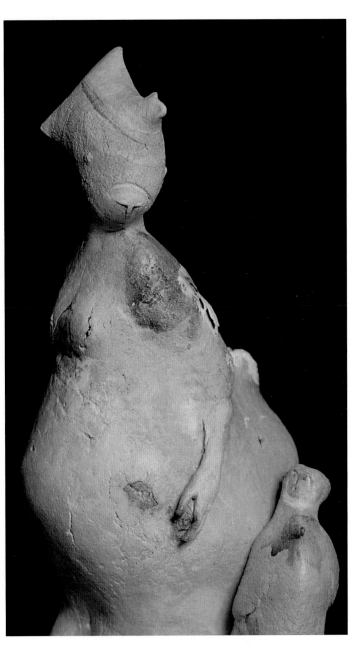

Bird Figure With Young II, (detail) 1997.
Height: 48 cm (18 ¾ in.).
Photograph by Nigel Collins.

Bird Figure With Young III, 1998.
Height: 43 cm (16 ¾ in.).
Photograph by Nigel Collins.

Crouching Bird Figure III, 1999.
Height: 52 cm (20 ½ in.).
Photograph by Nigel Collins.

Buonagurio, Toby

American. Born New York City (USA), 1947.

Since 1976 Senior Professor, New York State University, Stoneybrook. Since 1974 has exhibited frequently, mostly in New York. Collections include: American Crafts Museum, New York (USA); Mint Museum, Charlotte, North Carolina (USA). Lives and works in New York City (USA).

Bionic Toby with Pet Boa, 1982.
Ceramic with glazes and lustres,
height: 61 cm (24 in.).
Photograph by Edgar Buonagurio.

Neon-Idol (Dave),
1984.
Ceramic with glazes,
lustres, acrylic paint,
flocking, glitter and
lights,
213 x 157.5 x 73.5 cm
(84 x 62 x 29 in.).
Photograph by
Edgar Buonagurio.

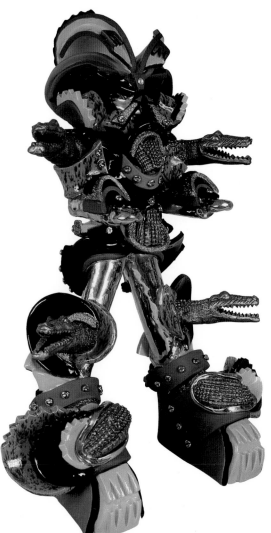

Robot with Alligators, 1985.
Glazed ceramic, lustres, paint.
62 x 51 x 25 cm
(24 ½ x 19 x 10 in.).
Photograph by Edgar Buonagurio.

Radiant Creatures of the Blue Coral Sea, 1990.
Ceramic with glazes, lustres, acrylic paint, flocking, and glitter.
61 x 208 x 56 cm
(24 x 82 x 22 in.).
Photograph by Edgar Buonagurio.

31

Burns, Mark

American. Born Springfield, Ohio (USA) 1950.

Represented by Frank Lloyd Gallery, CA; Ferrin Gallery, NY; Helen Drutt Gallery, PA (USA) (see appendix 2.). Collections include: Everson Museum, Syracuse, NY (USA); the Stedelijk, Amsterdam (see appendix 1). Lives and works in Philadelphia, Pennsylvania (USA).

Old Queen Teapot, 1998.
Slip-cast earthenware,
height: 39 cm (15 ½ in.).
Photograph courtesy of Garth
Clark Gallery, New York.

Frog Prince, 1998.
Slip-cast earthenware,
height: 33 cm (13 in.).
Photograph courtesy of Garth
Clark Gallery, New York.

Judgement of Paris, 1997.
Slip-cast earthenware,
height: 47 cm (18 ½ in.).
Photograph courtesy of Garth
Clark Gallery, New York.

Narcissus Cup, 1998.
Slip-cast earthenware,
height: 27 cm (10 ½ in.).
Photograph courtesy of
Garth Clark Gallery,
New York.

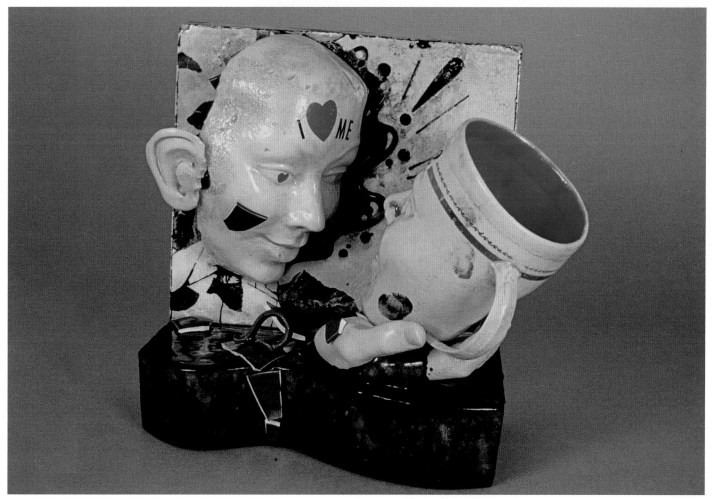

Capron, Roger

French. Born Paris (F), 1922.

Worked as a craftsman potter in Vallauris/Nizza (F) from 1942–52. Between then and 1982 he ran a small factory in Vallauris initially producing Provençal pottery and later unique decorative tiles. Became an associate of Picasso during the 1960s. Has worked as a freelance artist in Vallauris since 1982. He is a member of the International Academy of Ceramics. Collections include: Musée National de Ceramique, Sèvres (F) (see appendix 1); Musée Picasso, (F).

Happy Crowd, 1996.
Raku-fired tiles.
160 x 200 cm (63 x 78 ¾ in.).

The Three Women, 1995.
Raku. 65 x 60 cm
(25 ½ x 23 ½ in.).

Super Corte Maggiore,
1995.
Raku, height:
47 cm (18 ½ in.).

Corregan, Daphné

French. Born Pittsburgh, Pennsylvania (USA), 1954.

Moved to France in 1971 where she studied at various art schools. Professor at l'Ecole d'Arts Plastiques de Monaco since 1989. Also works occasionally in bronze or glass. Began working figuratively in 1993. Exhibiting regularly since 1981, mostly in France. Collections include: Musée National d'Art Moderne, Paris (F) (see appendix 1); Musée des Arts Décoratifs, Paris (F). Lives and works in Draguignan (F).

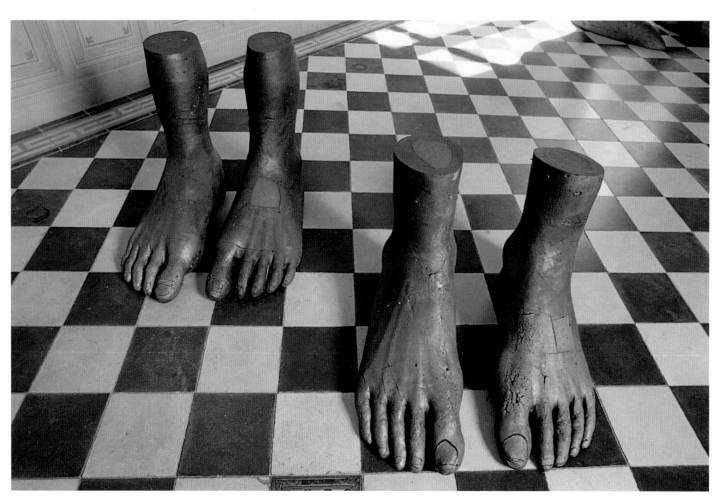

Black Feet, 1997.
Smoked ceramic, 60 x 60 cm (23 ½ x 23 ½ in.).

Femme Couchée, 1996.
25 x 45 cm (9 ¾ x 17 ¾ in.).

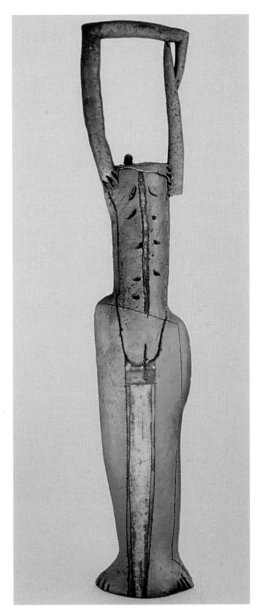

Femme Papillon,
1994.
Raku, height:
45 cm (17 ¾ in.).

Enfant Noir, 1995.
Smoked ceramic,
height: 65 cm
(25 ½ in.).

Tripoteuse, 1994.
Raku, height:
28 cm (11 in.).

Porteur, 1995.
Raku, height:
45 cm (17¾ in.).

Crowley, Jill

British. Born Cork (IRL), 1946.

One of the pioneers of New Ceramics in Britain in the 1970s. Internationally one of the best known ceramic artists. Collections include: Victoria and Albert Museum, London (GB); the Keramikmuseum Westerwald (D) (see appendix 1). Lives and works in London (GB).

Irish Man, 1979.
Stoneware, height: 36 cm (14 ¾ in.).

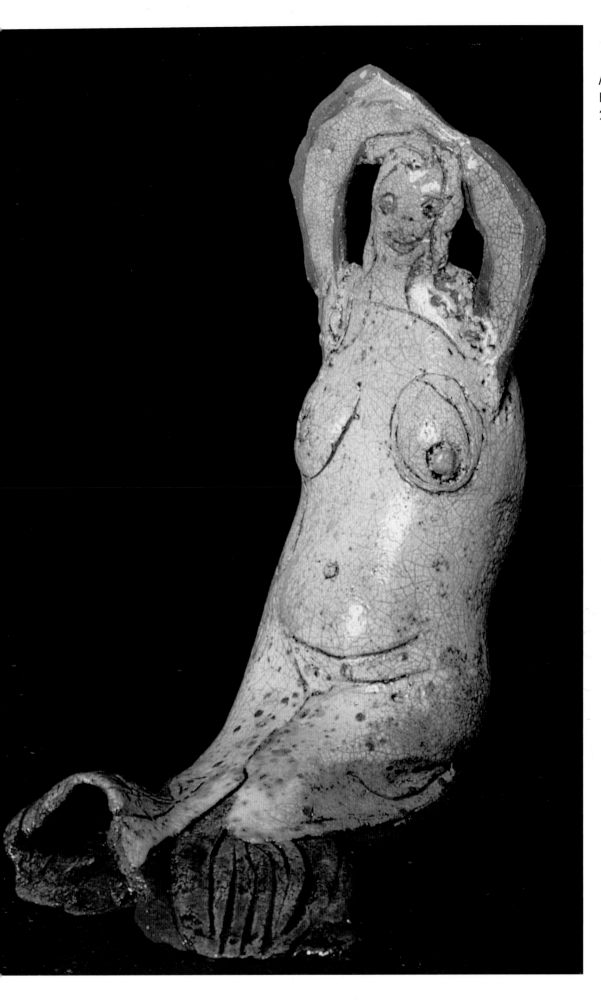

Mermaid, 1984.
Raku, height:
24 cm (9 ½ in.).

Smoked Hand, 1982–3.
Raku, height: 20 cm (8 in.).

Striped Arm, 1992.
Raku, 18 x 54 x 21 cm (7 x 21 ¼ x 8 ¼ in.).

Palm, 1999. Stoneware,
44 x 48 x 26 cm (17 ¼ x 19 x 10 ¼ in.).

Cut Off Man, 1979.
Stoneware, height: 53 cm (21 in.).

Curneen, Clare

Irish, Born Tralee, Co. Kerry (IRL), 1968.

Establishing a solid career mostly in Britain and Ireland since leaving MA course at Cardiff in 1992. Won the *Ceramic Monthly* (USA) International Sculptural Award in 1998. Collections include: Ulster Museum, Belfast (GB) (see appendix 1); Crawford Municipal Art Gallery, Cork (IRL). Lives and works in Cardiff, Wales (GB).

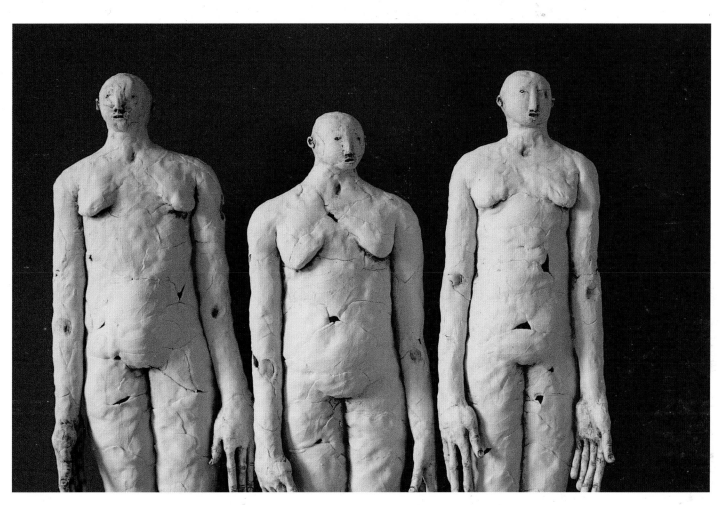

Standing Figures, 1997.
Porcelain, 60 x 17 x 10 cm (23 ½ x 6 ¾ x 4 in.).

RIGHT
Head, 1998.
Porcelain,
20 x 21 x 15 cm
(8 x 8 ¼ x 6 in.).

FAR RIGHT
Inside Out, 1998.
Porcelain,
40 x 30 x 20 cm
(15 ¾ x 11¾ x 8 in.).

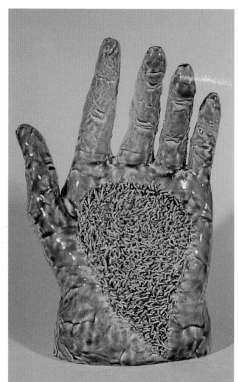

RIGHT
Standing Figure
(detail), 1995.
Porcelain, 55 x 18 cm
(21 ¾ x 7 in.).

FAR RIGHT
Standing Figure
(detail), 1995.
Porcelain, 55 x 18 cm
(21 ¾ x 7 in.).

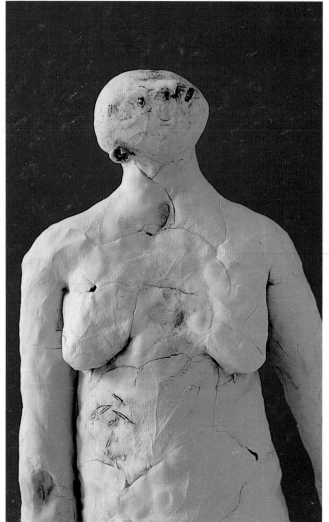

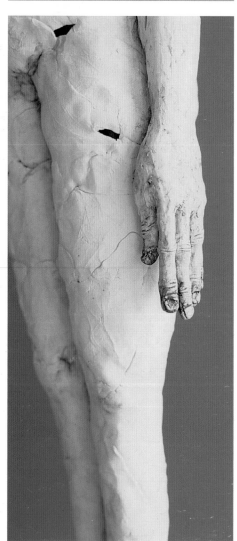

Cushway, David

British. Born Wickford, Essex (GB), 1965.

Concept rather than object oriented approach working with video, computer, unfired clay etc. His video installation *Sublimation* has toured widely in Britain and Europe. Lives and works in Cardiff, Wales (GB).

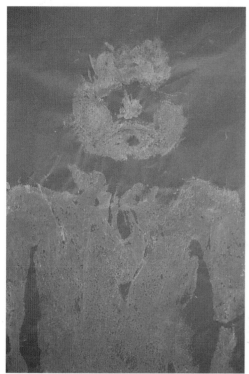

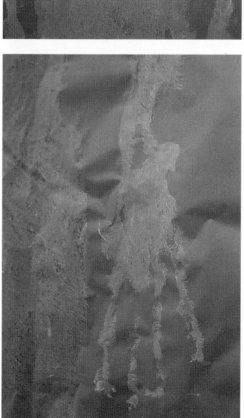

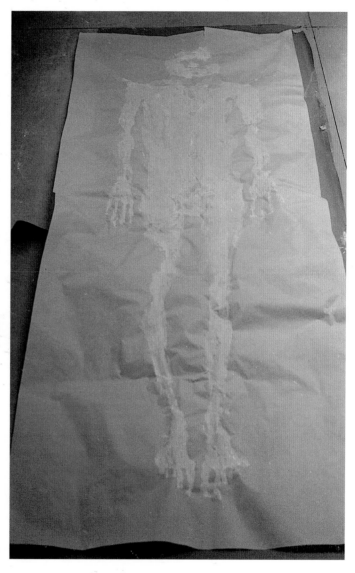

ABOVE LEFT   *Trace*, (detail) 1998.
Body print with porcelain on paper.
Height: approx. life-size.

LEFT   *Trace*, (detail)1998.
Body print with porcelain on paper.
Height: approx. life-size.

ABOVE   *Trace*, 1998.
Body print with porcelain on paper.
Height: approx. life-size.

Sublimation, 1999. A sequence of stills
from video, showing the disintegration
of a life-size clay head.

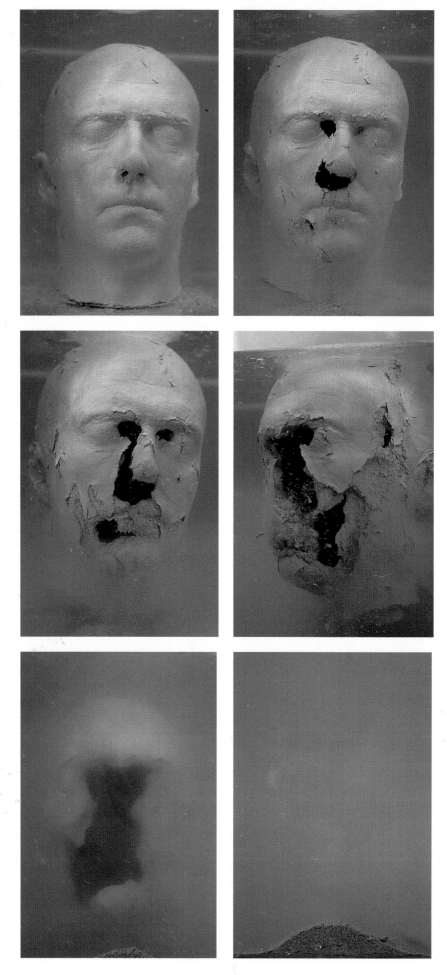

de Staebler, Stephen

American. Born Saint Louis, Missouri (USA), 1933.

Began exhibiting his distinctive, monumental clay or bronze forms, (which can be up to 367 cm/144 in. tall) after completing an MA at the University of California, Berkeley in 1961. Played a seminal role in the development of sculptural ceramics in America. He has done many site specific sculptures, mostly in California. Collections include: San Francisco Museum of Modern Art, San Francisco (USA); Minneapolis Institute of Arts, Minneapolis (USA). Represented by Franklin Parrasch Gallery, New York (see appendix 2). Lives and works in Berkeley, California (USA).

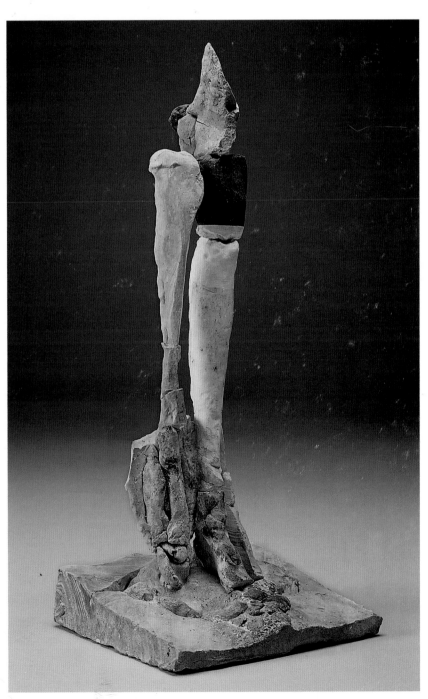

LEFT
Right-Sided Woman Standing, 1979.
230 x 30.5 x 30.5 cm (90 ½ x 12 x 12 in.).
Photograph courtesy of Franklin Parrasch Gallery, New York.

RIGHT
Two Legs with Black Knee, 1997–8.
89 x 39 x 35.5 cm (35 ¼ x 15 ½ x 14 in.).
Photograph courtesy of Franklin Parrasch Gallery, New York.

*Two Legs with Red Splint,*1996–8.
Fired clay and wood,
84 x 30.5 x 25.5 cm
(33 ¼ x 12 x 10 ¼ in.).
Photograph courtesy of Franklin Parrasch
Gallery, New York.

Seated Figure with Striped Right Arm, (detail), 1984.
Height: 185 cm (73 in.).
Photograph by Michael Flynn, courtesy of Franklin Parrasch Gallery, New York.

Standing Figure with Segmented Knee, (detail), 1983.
Height: 235.5 cm (92 ¾ in.).
Photo by Michael Flynn, courtesy of Franklin Parrasch Gallery, New York.

Standing Figure with Quartered Torso, (detail), 1985.
Height: 236 cm (93 in.).
Photograph by Michael Flynn, courtesy of Franklin Parrasch Gallery, New York.

Standing Figure with Quartered Torso, (detail), 1985.
Height: 236 cm (93 in.).
Photograph by Michael Flynn, courtesy of Franklin Parrasch Gallery, New York.

Dietz, Gundi

Austrian. Born Vienna (A), 1942.

Probably the best known Austrian ceramic artist. Work varies widely from large mixed-media pieces to tiny porcelain figures. Member of the International Academy of Ceramics (see p.233). Collections include: Cooper Hewitt Museum, New York (USA) (see appendix 1); the Museum of Applied Arts, Vienna (A). Lives and works in Enzersdorf (A).

Porcelain Figures, 1998.
Porcelain, height: 10 cm (4 in.).

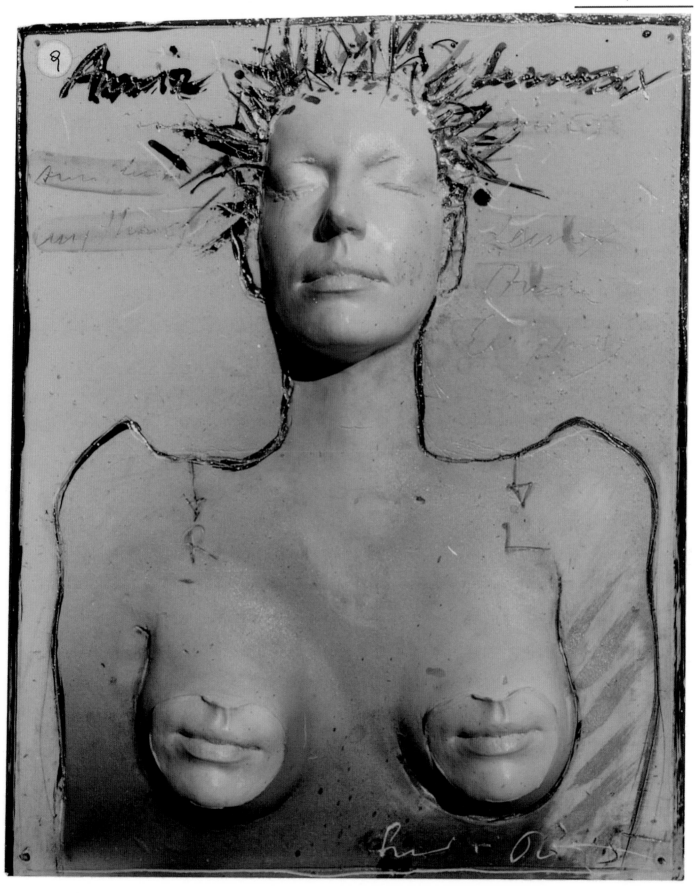

Baserschalen – Ihre Lippen, 1993.
Porcelain, 50 x 40 cm (19 ¾ x 15 ¾ in.).

Body, 1974.
Porcelain, height: 30 cm (11 ¾ in.).

Body, 1974.
Porcelain, height: 30 cm (11 ¾ in.).

Strong Women, 1989–91.
Porcelain/mixed media, height: approx. life-size.

Dionyse, Carmen

Belgian. Born Ghent (B), 1921.

A figure of enormous standing in Europe, having received many awards and prizes including titles from the King of Belgium. Has exhibited throughout Europe regularly since 1956. Collections include: Royal Museum of Contemporary Art, Brussels (B); Bellerive Museum, Zürich (CH) (see appendix 1). Member of the International Academy of Ceramics (see p.233). Lives and works in Ghent (B).

Vitriol II, 1991–2.
Height: 89 cm (35 in.).

Vanitas, 1993.
Height: 53 cm (21 in.).

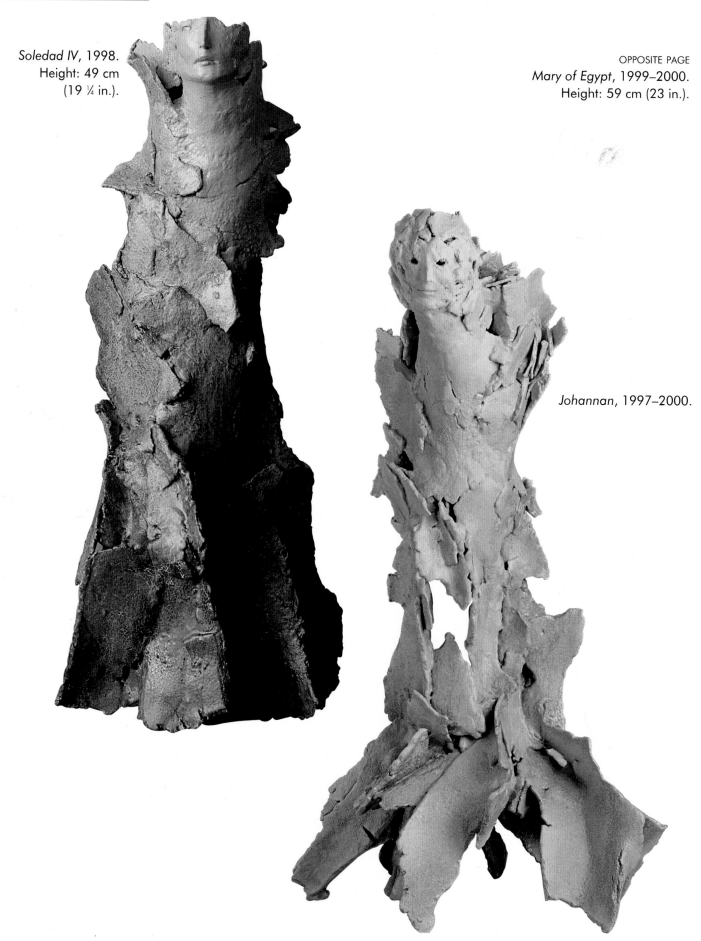

Soledad IV, 1998.
Height: 49 cm
(19 ¼ in.).

OPPOSITE PAGE
Mary of Egypt, 1999–2000.
Height: 59 cm (23 in.).

Johannan, 1997–2000.

Dixon, Stephen

British. Born Peterlee, Co. Durham (GB), 1957.

Shows regularly throughout Britain and sometimes in USA since leaving the Royal College of Art, London (GB) in 1986. Represented by Nancy Margolis in USA (see appendix 2). Collections include: the Mint Museum, Charlotte, North Carolina (USA) (see appendix 1); the British Council (GB). Lives and works in Manchester (GB).

Five More Years, 1992.
Earthenware, height: 58 cm (22 ¾ in.).
Photograph by Lee Avison .

FAR LEFT
Dixon's Menagerie,
1995.
Earthenware, height:
52 cm (20 ½ in.).
Photograph by Richard
Weltman.

LEFT
Godiva, 1992.
Earthenware, height:
21 cm (8 ¼ in.).
Photograph by Len Grant.

BELOW LEFT AND
DETAIL RIGHT
Bare Ladies, 1998.
Earthenware, height:
27 cm (10 ½ in.).
Photograph by Joel Fildes.

Earl, Jack

American. Born Unipolis, Ohio (USA), 1934.

Leading figure in American ceramics for over 30 years. Represented by Nancy Margolis Gallery, New York and Perimeter Gallery, Chicago (see appendix 2). Collections include: Art Institute of Chicago, Chicago, Illinois (USA); Smithsonian Institution, Washington DC (USA) (see appendix 1). Lives and works in Unipolis, Ohio, USA.

Bill Builds a Ruin, 1999.
Earthenware.
23 x 19 x 49 cm
(9 x 7 ½ x 19 ¼ in.).

Bill Went to Town and Got a Hair Cut,
1995.
Earthenware, 47 x 43 x 25.5 cm
(18 ½ x 17 x 10 in.).

Eglin, Philip

British. Born Gibraltar (GBZ), 1959.

Teaches at North Staffordshire University (GB). Has achieved a high profile in Britain since winning Jerwood Prize in 1997. Exhibits regularly in Britain and also at the Garth Clark Gallery in New York (see appendix 2). Collections include: the Victoria and Albert Museum, London (GB); the Stedlijk Museum, Amsterdam (NL) (see appendix 1). Lives and works in Stoke-on-Trent (GB).

Recumbent Nude, 1999.
23 x 33 cm (9 x 13 in.).
Photograph courtesy of Garth Clark Gallery, New York.

The Seated Virgin,
1999.
Earthenware,
23 x 33 cm
(9 x 13 in.).
Photograph courtesy
of Garth Clark
Gallery, New York.

Fekete, Laszlo

Hungarian. Born Budapest (H), 1949.

Exhibits throughout Europe and with Garth Clark in USA (see appendix 2). Member of the International Academy of Ceramics (see p.233). Collections include: Janos Pannonius Museum, Pecs (H); International Ceramic Museum, Kecskemét (H) (see appendix 1). Lives and works in Budapest (H).

Half-God Half Bloodness and
Half-Blood, Half Goddess, 1999.
Porcelain.

Iron-Clay Gods, 1993.
Coloured clay, height: (tallest) 52.5 cm (20 ½ in.).

Head of Heads (detail) 1986.
Coloured clay, height: 85 cm (33 ½ in.).

Horn of Plenty, 1997.
Porcelain, height: 60 cm (23 ½ in.).

LEFT
Relic from the End of XX Century, 1992.
Coloured clay, height: 150 cm (60 in.).

Superman's Mortal Combat, 1999. Porcelain, height: 40 cm (15 ¾ in.).

Fell, Fiona

Australian. Born Lismore, New South Wales (AUS), 1966.

Well-known and frequent exhibitor in Australia. Collections include: the Power House Museum, Sydney (AUS); the Taipei Fine Arts Museum (TW) (see appendix 1).

Hedge Huddling, 1997.
Earthenware,
32 x 30 x 18 cm
(12.5 x 12 x 7 in.).

Haughty Their Array, 1996.
Earthenware, 52 x 33 x 23 cm
(20 ½ x 13 x 9 in.).

Exile, 1996.
Earthenware, 74 x 50 cm (29 x 19 ½ in.).

Stealth, 1996.
Earthenware,
37 x 41 x 12 cm
(14 ½ x 16 x 4 ¾ in.).

Fischer, Lothar

German. Born Gemersheim Pfalz (D),1933.

From 1975–97, Professor at the Hochschule der Künste, Berlin. Although his favoured medium is cast-iron, he also works in bronze, aluminium and plaster and has produced large numbers of ceramic sculptures. These pieces are hollow-formed and unglazed although occasionally painted, usually by an artist friend at his invitation. Has produced many site-specific sculptures, in various materials, throughout Germany. Collections include: the New National Gallery, Berlin (D); the Kröller-Müller Museum (NL). Lives and works in Berlin and in Baierbrun bei München (D).

Peasant Dance, 1964.
Unglazed ceramic,
57 x 46 x 15 cm (22 ¼ x 18 x 6 in.).

Susanna in Bath, 1964.
Terracotta, 35 x 30 x 20 cm
(13 ¾ x 11 ¾ x 8 in.).

Kneeling I, 1971.
Unglazed ceramic,
39 x 20 x 21cm
(15 ¼ x 8 x 8 ¼ in.).

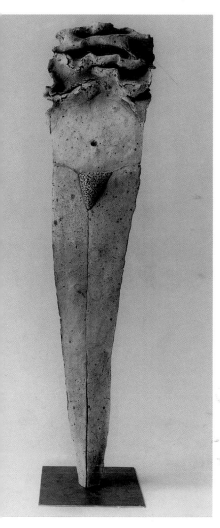

ABOVE
Strip-tease I, 1973.
101 x 25 x 8 cm
(39 ¾ x 9 ¾ x 3 in.).

ABOVE CENTRE
Dolores Bathing, 1967.
75 x 98 x 40 cm
(29 ¾ x 38 ¾ x 15 ¾ in.).

ABOVE
*Woman Carrying an
Animal,* 1993.
66 x 20 x 8 cm
(26 x 8 x 3 in.).

LEFT
Little Scissor Woman,
1987.
26 x 8 x 3 cm
(8 ¼ x 4 x ¾ in.)

Transparent Couple, 1987.
Fired clay and wire, 65 x 35 x 40 cm
(25 ¾ x 13 ¾ x 15 ¾ in.).

Fischer, Wayne

American. Born Milwaukee, Wisconsin (USA), 1953.

Worked as a potter and sculptor in Milwaukee and Boston after leaving the University of Wisconsin in 1976. Moved to France in 1986. Also makes wide range of functional ware. Collections include: Boston Museum of Fine Art (USA) (see appendix 1); Byers Museum, Chicago (USA). Lives and works in Revest les Eaux (F).

Untitled No.I, 1998.
Porcelain,
71 x 50 x 36 cm
(28 x 20 x 14 in.).

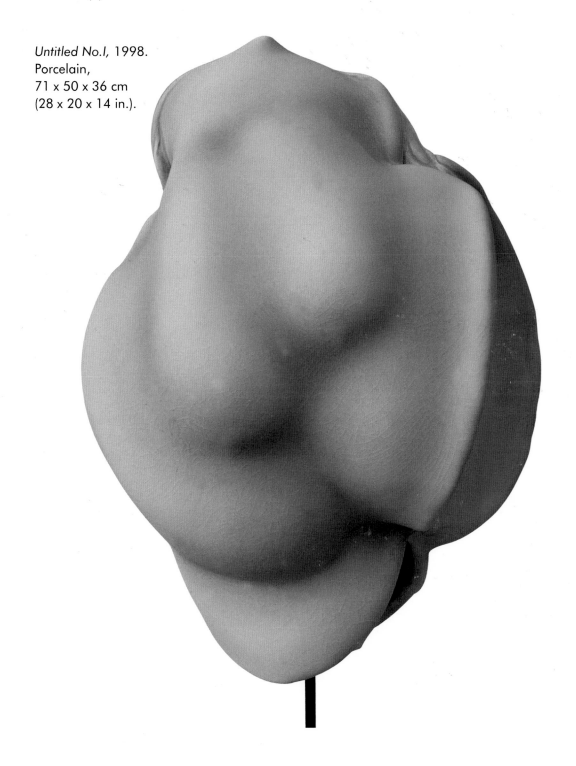

RIGHT
Untitled No. 3,
1997.
Porcelain,
49 x 47 x 22 cm
(19 ¼ x 18 ½ x 8 ¾ in.).

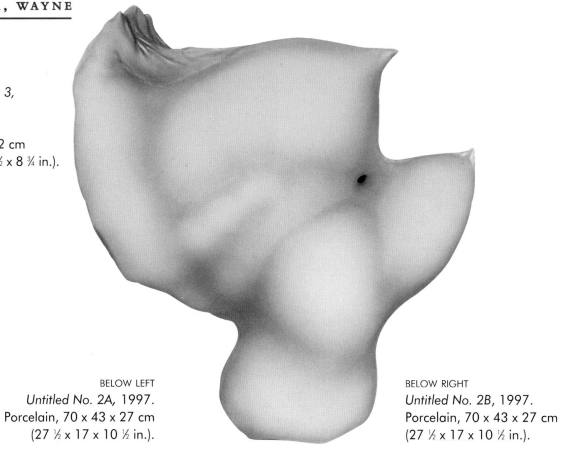

BELOW LEFT
Untitled No. 2A, 1997.
Porcelain, 70 x 43 x 27 cm
(27 ½ x 17 x 10 ½ in.).

BELOW RIGHT
Untitled No. 2B, 1997.
Porcelain, 70 x 43 x 27 cm
(27 ½ x 17 x 10 ½ in.).

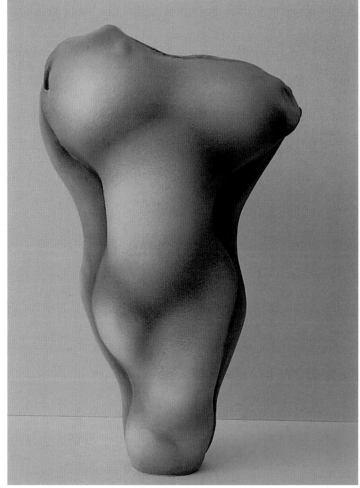

Flynn, Michael

British/Irish. Born Wuppertal (D), 1947.

Exhibits frequently all over the world. Represented by Franklin Parrasch Gallery in USA (see appendix 2). Member of the International Academy of Ceramics (see p.233). Has completed several site-specific commissions in Holland and Britain. Collections include:Victoria and Albert Museum, London (GB);Virginia Museum of Fine Arts, Richmond,Virginia (USA) (see appendix 1). Lives and works in Cardiff, Wales (GB) and Vallendar/Höhr-Grenzhausen (D).

Courtship, 1998.
Raku, height: 51 cm (20 ½ in.).
Photograph courtesy of Franklin Parrasch Gallery, New York.

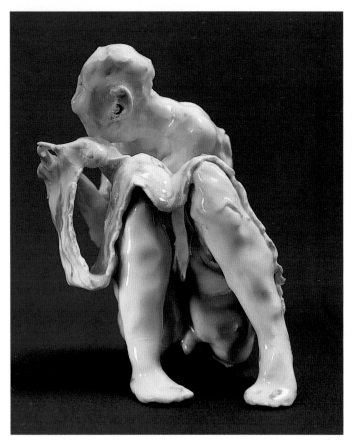

Knitting, 1999.
Porcelain, height: 20 cm (8 in.).
Photograph courtesy of Mint museum, North Carolina.

Angel Flight, 1988.
Raku fired clay with concrete base, height: 60 cm (23 ½ in.).
Photograph courtesy of the Board of Trustees of the Victoria and Albert Museum Picture Library, London.

The Sofa, 2000.
Porcelain, height: 35 cm (13 ¾ in.).
Photograph courtesy of Franklin Parrasch Gallery, New York.

Acrobat, 1997.
Stoneware, height: 42 cm (16 ½ in.),
Photograph courtesy of Franklin Parrasch Gallery, New York.

Ship of Fools, 2000.
Porcelain, 32 x 45 cm (12 ½ x 17 ¾ in.).

Fontana, Lucio

Argentinian. Born Rosano, Santa Fe (ARG), 1899.

Known especially for his slash canvasses/metal sheets of the late 1950s/early 1960s, but working in a wide variety of media, became internationally known from that period onwards. One of the first to seek an art form belonging neither to painting nor to sculpture through the use of ceramic. He worked at the Sèvres Factory in France in 1937 and founded the Spazialismo movement in Milan in 1947. His ceramic work includes the large, pierced spheres of his *Nature* series, his spacial ceramics and a great many animal and human figures from 12 cm (4 ¾ in.) high to around 170 cm (67 in.) high. Died Cornabbio, Varese (I) 1968.

Cotta Figure, c.1940.
Terracotta, height: 18.5 cm (7 ¼ in.).
Photograph courtesy of Garth Clark Gallery, New York.

Crucifixion, 1950–55.
30.5 x 17 x 9.5 cm (12 x 6 ¾ x 3 ¾ in.).
Photograph courtesy of Garth Clark Gallery, New York.

Frank, Mary

American. Born London (GB), 1933.

Emigrated to the USA in 1940. A pioneer of the new figurative movement in ceramics in the 1970s along with Arneson, Frey and de Staebler. Works in a variety of media but has concentrated on painting in the last few years. Lives and works in New York City (USA). Represented by D.C. Moore Gallery, New York, USA (see apppendix 2). Collections include: Whitney Museum of American Art, New York, USA (see appendix 1).

Persephone, 1985.
Terracotta, 71 x 185 x 101.5 cm (28 x 73 x 40 in.).

Standing Woman, 1978.
Ceramic in two parts, 98 x 53 x 55 cm (38 ½ x 21 x 22 in.).

Lover, 1977.
59.5 x 112 x 63.5 cm
(23 x 44 x 25 in.).

BELOW LEFT
Messenger, 1991–92.
Collage and oil on
board, 122 x 244 cm
(48 x 96 in.).

RIGHT
Head with Shadow,
1981.
Height: 89 cm (35 in.).

Frey, Viola

American. Born Lodi, California (USA), 1933.

Since the 1960s a pioneer in redefining the tradition of figurative ceramic art in the USA. Professor, California College of Arts and Crafts, Oakland (USA), since 1970. Represented by the Nancy Hoffman Gallery in New York (see appendix 2). Work in most major museums and collections in USA (see appendix 1). Lives and works in Oakland, California (USA).

Studio View, 1993.
Photograph by John Wilson White, courtesy of Nancy Hoffman Gallery, New York.

OPPOSITE
Roman Market Woman & The Big Hand, 1988.
167.5 x 84 x 91.5 cm (66 x 33 x 36 in.).
Photograph courtesy of Nancy Hoffman Gallery, New York.

TOP
World Culture Bricolage 1999.
78.5 x 162.5 x 46 cm (31 x 64 x 18 in.).
Photograph by Michael Flynn, courtesy of Nancy Hoffman Gallery, New York.

BOTTOM
Resting Woman, 1988–89.
105 x 271.5 x 127 cm (41 ½ x 107 x 50 in.).
Photograph courtesy of Nancy Hoffman Gallery, New York.

RIGHT
Man, 1982.
276.5 x 86.5 x 63.5 cm
(109 x 34 x 25 in.).
Photograph courtesy
of Nancy Hoffman
Gallery, New York.

FAR RIGHT
Artist's Left Glove,
1987.
153.5 x 99 x 81 cm
(60 ½ x 39 x 32 in.).
Photograph courtesy
of Nancy Hoffman
Gallery, New York.

RIGHT
World Civilization 3,
1987.
145 x 59 x 41 cm
(57 x 23 x 16 in.).
Photograph courtesy
of Nancy Hoffman
Gallery, New York.

FAR RIGHT
*Standing Woman with
Yellow Cheek*, 1999.
236 x 63.5 x 48 cm
(93 x 25 x 19 in.).
Photograph courtesy
of Nancy Hoffman
Gallery, New York.

Fuller, Geoffrey

British. Born Chesterfield, Derbyshire (GB), 1936.

His vessels and figurines, referring directly to traditional British ceramic history, are well-known in Britain. Collections include: Victoria and Albert Museum, London (GB); Leicester Museum and Art Gallery (GB) (see appendix 1). Lives and works in Derbyshire (GB).

Herne The Hunter, 1985.
Earthenware, height: 35.5 cm (14 in.).

Couple On Bench, 1992.
Earthenware, height: 35.5 cm (14 in.).

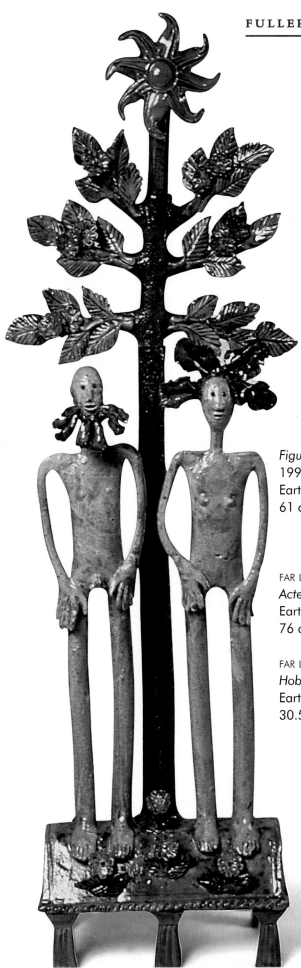

Figures Under a Tree,
1995.
Earthenware, height:
61 cm (24 in.).

FAR LEFT, ABOVE
Acteon, 1996.
Earthenware, height:
76 cm (30 in.).

FAR LEFT, BELOW
Hobby Horse, 1997.
Earthenware, height:
30.5 cm (12 in.).

Fusz, Geörgy

Hungarian. Born Szekzárd (H), 1955.

Lecturer at the Academy of Applied Arts, Budapest since 1987. Collections: the Applied Arts Collection of Kanton Bern (CH); Janos Pannonius Museum, Pecs (H). Lives and works in Budapest and in Szekzárd (H).

ABOVE
Transformation, 1992.
Porcelain, height:
47 cm (18 ½ in.).

ABOVE RIGHT
Decaying, 1981.
Coal-fired, height:
60 cm (23 ½ in.).

RIGHT
Blue Boy, 1992.
Stoneware, height:
160 cm (63 in.).

FAR RIGHT
Dragon Boy, 1992.
Stoneware, height:
95 cm (37 ¼ in.).

RIGHT
The Gift, 1994.
Stoneware, height:
60 cm (23 ½ in.).

BELOW LEFT
Loki, 1998.
Stoneware, height:
120 cm (47 ¾ in.).

CENTRE
Alone, 1998.
Stoneware, height:
38 cm (15 in.).

BELOW
Clown, 1998.
Stoneware, height:
32 cm (12 ½ in.).

Geszler, Maria

Hungarian. Born Budapest (H), 1941.

A pioneer of modern Ceramics in Hungary. Her work is very well-known throughout Europe.
Member of the International Academy of Ceramics (see p.233). Collections include:
Keramikmuseum Westerwald (D); Museum of Applied Art, Budapest (H) (see appendix 1).
Lives and works in Szombathely (H).

Utomaro's Factory, 1998.
Porcelain with silkscreen print,
81 x 39 x 20 cm (32 x 15 ¼ x 8 in.).

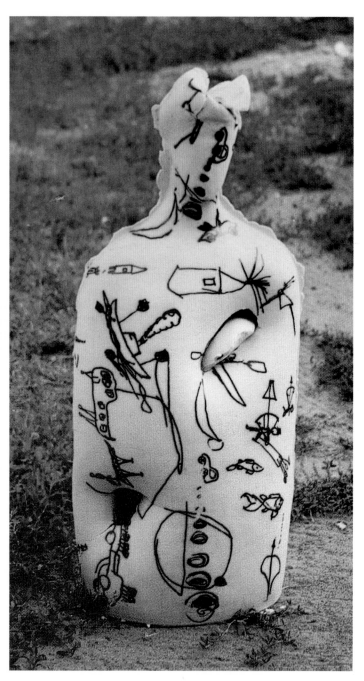

Hommage à Garzuly Gábor, 1997.
Porcelain with silkscreen print.
72 x 34 x 21 cm (28 ¼ x 13 ½ x 8 ¼ in.).

Glave, Patricia

Swiss/French. Born Bâsle (CH).

Collections include: Mino Museum (JAP); Johannes Jakob Museum, Zürich (CH).
Lives and works in Lausanne (CH).

RIGHT
Fragments,
(detail),1996.
Stoneware, height:
150 cm (60 in.).
.

BELOW LEFT
Fragments, 1996.
Stoneware, height:
150 cm (60 in.).

BELOW CENTRE
Fragments, 1996,
(in Studio Lausanne).
Porcelain, height:
180 cm (71 in.).

BELOW
Fragments, 1996.
Stoneware, height:
150 cm (60 in.).

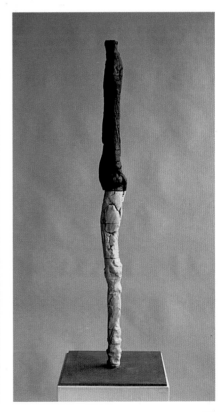

Gonzalez, Arthur

American. Born Sacremento, California (USA), 1954.

Associate Professor, California College of the Arts since 1991. Highly active on the American West Coast ceramic scene. Frequent exhibitions since completing MFA at University of California, Davis in 1981. Represented by the John Natsoulas Gallery and John Elder Gallery in USA (see appendix 2). Collections include: the American Craft Museum, New York (USA) (see appendix 1); Rutgers University, New Brunswick, NJ (USA). Several site-specific commissions in California. Lives and works in Almeda, California (USA).

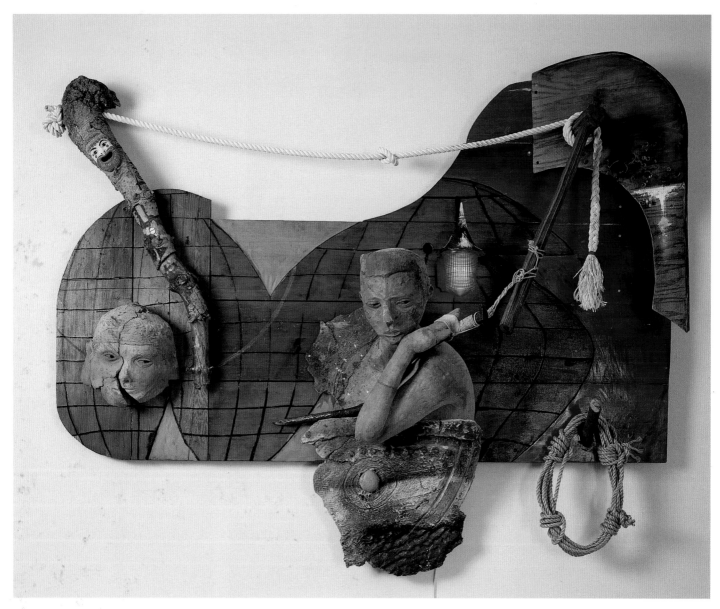

Travelog, 1989.
Clay, wood, rope, light fixture, 127 x 203 x 41 cm (50 x 80 x 16 in.).

ABOVE
Le Grande Attack,
1984.
Photograph courtesy of
the Shape Gallery.

RIGHT
Untitled, 1995.
Clay, oil painting,
wood,
66 x 91.5 x 50 cm
(26 x 36 x 20 in.).

RIGHT
At Heart Level, 1992.
Clay, steel, wood,
160 x 89 x 53 cm
(63 x 35 x 21 in.).

FAR RIGHT
Noir, 1987.
Fired clay, antler,
dishrag,
127 x 84 x 50 cm
(50 x 33 x 20 in.).

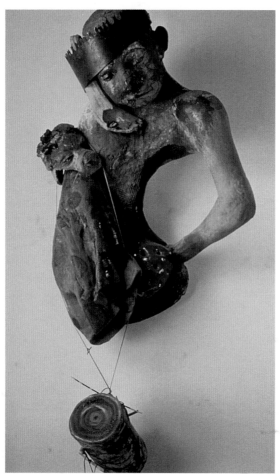

RIGHT
Lap Dance, 1997.
Glazed and fired clay,
63.5 x 28 x 15 cm
(25 x 11 x 6 in.).

FAR RIGHT
Borderland, 1998.
Clay, glass,
160 x 162.5 x 56 cm
(63 x 64 x 22 in.).

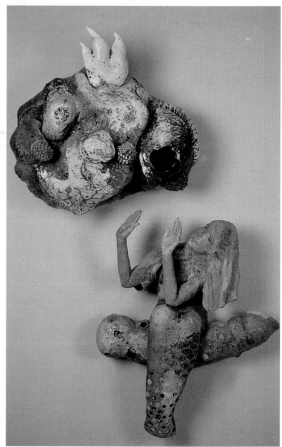

Grzimek, Jana

German. Born Berlin (D), 1964.

Often works in other media: bronze, plaster, and also two-dimensions. More recently has produced several series of figures in maiolica or in porcelain. Has made several site-specific pieces in Berlin. Collections include: Museum Unser Liebe Frau, Magdeburg (D); Worpswede Museum (D). Lives and works in Berlin (D).

Group of Argonauts, (detail) 1996.
Faience, height: 26 cm (10 ¼ in.).
Photograph by Joachim Fliegner.

Group of Argonauts, (detail) 1996.
Faience, height: 26 cm (10 ¼ in.).
Photograph by Joachim Fliegner.

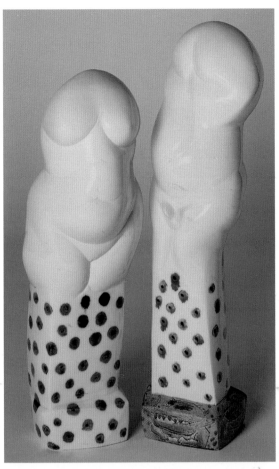

FAR LEFT
Venus and Adonis,
1992.
Porcelain,
33 x 37cm
(13 x 14 ½ in.).
Photograph by
Joachim Fliegner.

LEFT
Birth of the East,
1998–9.
Height: 180 cm
(71 in.).

FAR LEFT
Klytemnastra's Revenge, 1995.
Faience, height:
55 cm x (25 ½ in.).
Photograph by
Joachim Fliegner.

LEFT
Ceramic Column in Katharinenklosterhof,
1990.
Height: 240 cm
(94 ½ in.).
Photograph by
Uwe Podratz.

Haug, Nica

German. Born Memmingen (D), 1958.

Exhibits mostly in Bavaria. Collections include: The Bavarian Convention, Munich (D); Museum of Ceramics, Bechynê (CZ) (see appendix 1). Lives and works in Überlingen (D).

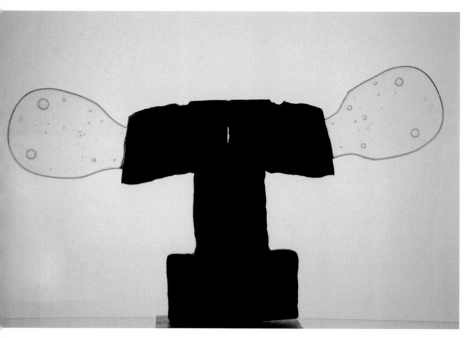

Winged Figure, 1990.
Stoneware and wire, 27 x 30 x 10 cm
(10 ½ x 11 ¾ x 4 in.).
Photo courtesy of Gallery B15, Munich.

Winged Figure, 1989.
Stoneware, 38 x 32 x 7 cm (15 x 12 ½ x 2 ¾ in.).
Photo courtesy of Gallery B15, Munich.

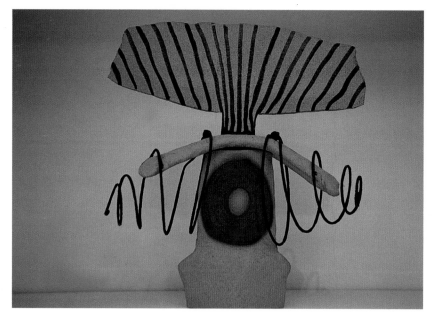

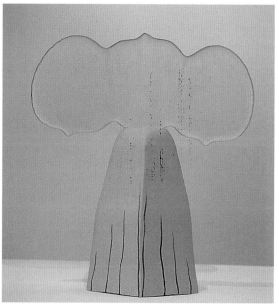

Winged Figure, 1990.
Ceramic and wire, 26 x 25 x 8 cm (10 ¼ x 9 ¾ x 3 ¼ in.).
Photo courtesy of Gallery B15, Munich.

Winged Figure, 1990.
Stoneware and glass, 37 x 31 x 10 cm (14 ½ x 12 x 4 i
Photo courtesy of Gallery B15, Munich.

Hebenstreit, Theresia

German. Born Wiesbaden (D), 1950.

Her work is very popular in Germany. Collections include: Baden-Württembergisches Landesmuseum, Stuttgart (D) (see appendix 1); Siegburg Museum, Nordrhein-Westfalen (D). Lives and works in Wiesbaden (D).

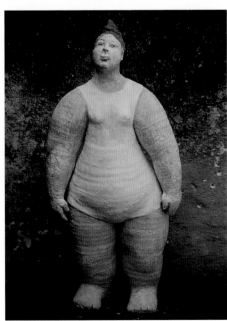

TOP
Wally Gree Nude, 1998.
Height: 34 cm (13 ½ in.).

BOTTOM
Trudchen, 1998.
Height: 56 cm (22 in.).

TOP
Anne True Love, 1998.
Height: 33 cm (13 in.).

BOTTOM
Pomona, 1998.
Height: 72 cm (28 ¼ in.).

Held, Marion

American. Born New York City (USA),

Highly active and innovative sculptor using a wide variety of media. Frequent exhibitions, mostly in the New York/New Jersey area. Collections include: New Jersey State Museum, Trenton, NJ (USA); University of Beer Sheva (ISR) (see appendix 1). Lives and works in Montclair, New Jersey (USA).

Memorial Series: Open, 1998.
Rubber, ceramic, wood, water, 35.5 x 19 x 51 cm (14 x 7.5 x 20 in.).

OPPOSITE
Proboscis, 1999.
Rubber, latex, stoneware and wire, 38 x 16.5 x 43 cm (15 x 6.5 x 17 in.).

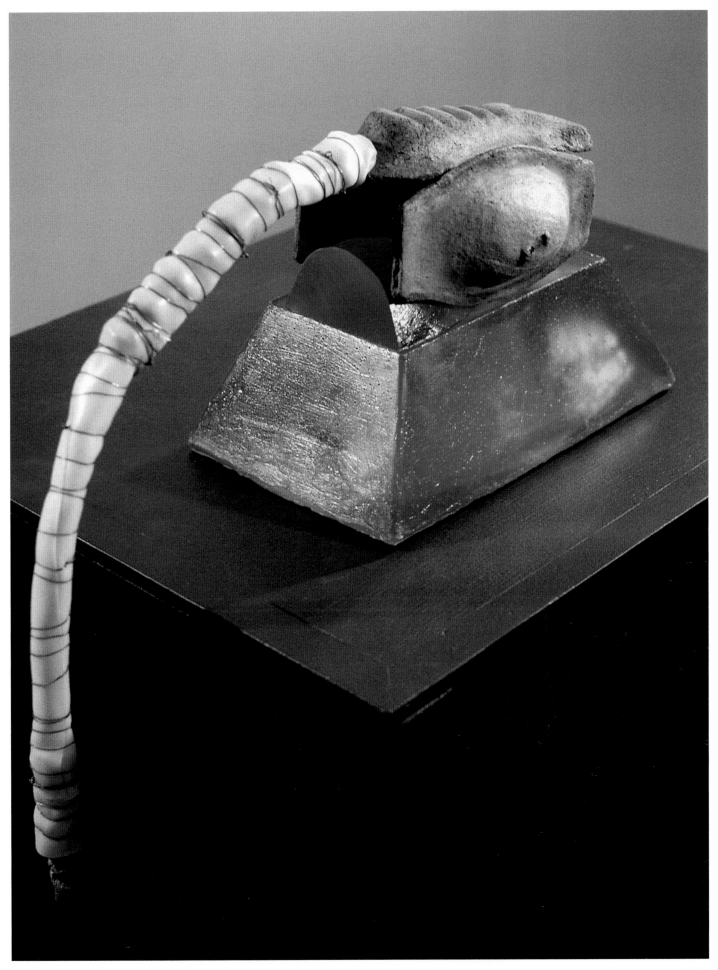

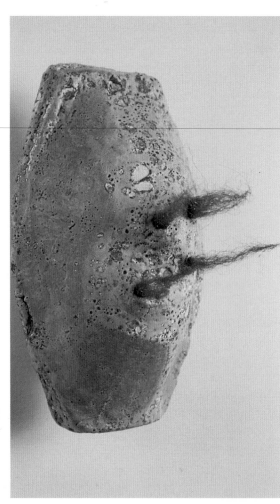

FAR LEFT
Homage to Ex Voto II,
1991–2.
Stoneware, wood,
94 x 99 x 259 cm
(37 x 39 x 102 in.).

LEFT
Skin, 1996.
Stoneware and brillo,
19 x 11.5 x 15 cm
(7.5 x 4.5 x 6 in.).

FAR LEFT
Reaching Figure, 1989.
Stoneware,
119 x 114.5 x 43 cm
(47 x 45 x 17 in.).

LEFT
Guardian of the Parts,
1998.
Mixed media,
172.5 x 101.5 x 53 cm
(68 x 40 x 21in.).

Henry, Sean

British. Born Woking, Surrey (GB), 1965.

Most figures are around, but never quite life-size, in fired and painted ceramic or painted bronze. Represented by the John Natsoulas Gallery in (USA); Berkeley Square Gallery, London (GB) (see appendix 2). Collections include: Sculpture at Goodwood (GB) (see appendix 1); Hilton Hotel, Ankara (TRK). Lives and works in London (GB).

Lying Man, 1999.
Fired clay, oil paint, perspex, wood.
Figure: 125 x 51 x 53 cm (49 x 20 x 21 in.),
base: 135 x 66 x 110 cm (53 x 26 x 43 in.).

ABOVE
Mermaid, 1990,
(commission).
Height: 153 cm
(60 in.).
Photograph courtesy of
John Natsoulas Gallery,
California.

ABOVE RIGHT
Mermaid, (detail) 1990,
(specific commission).
Height: 153 cm
(60 in.).
Photograph courtesy of
John Natsoulas Gallery,
California.

RIGHT
London Fields, 1995.
Ceramic and oil paint,
81 x 41 x 20 cm
(32 x 16 x 8 in.).
Photograph courtesy of
John Natsoulas Gallery,
California.

Bob Marley, 1991.
Painted ceramic, height: approx. life-size.
Photograph courtesy of John Natsoulas Gallery,
California.

Heyes, Tracey

British, Born Doncaster (GB), 1964.

Teaches at Bretton Hall College, University of Leeds (GB). Collections: Shigaraki Cultural Park (JAP). Has been involved in a large number of site-specific commissions in England. Lives and works in Sheffield (GB).

BELOW
Untitled, 1996.
Earthenware on bronzed mirror,
100 x 55 cm (39 ½ x 22 in.).

RIGHT
Untitled, 1992.
Reduced stoneware, wire lacing,
height: 73cm (28 ¾ in.).

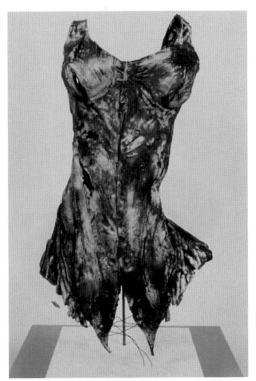

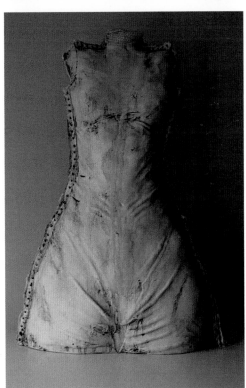

FAR LEFT
Untitled, 1995.
Reduced stoneware
with impressed letters,
height: 70 cm
(27 ½ in.).

LEFT
Untitled, 1997.
Eartheware glass
beads, stains and
oxides, height:
85 cm (33 ½ in.).

Untitled, 1995.
Wall piece, muslin lined, leather lacing, 30 x 60 x 15 cm (11 ¾ x 23 ½ x 6 in.).

Hole, Nina

Danish. Born Fyn (DK), 1941.

Co-founder of Clay Today International Ceramic Centre, Gulagegaard (DK). Known for her spectacular on-site firings of huge 'house' forms. Member of the International Academy of Ceramics (see p.233). Collections include: Museum of Art and Industry, Copenhagen (DK); Aberystwyth Arts Centre, Wales (GB) (see appendix 1). Lives and works in Skaelskor (DK).

Adriadne, 1996.
Low-fired, height: 30 cm (11 ¾ in.).

Pythia, 1997.
Low-fired, height: 50 cm (20 in.).

Aphrodite, 1997.
Low-fired, height:
30 cm (11 ¾ in.).

Hoys, Marnix

Belgian. Born Bruges (B), 1943.

Extremely active, exhibiting and teaching in Belgium for over 30 years. Member of the International Academy of Ceramics (see p.233). Several site-specific commissions in Flanders. Collections include: Hessichen Landesmuseum, Darmstadt (D); Museum of Decorative Arts, Ghent (B) (see appendix 1). Lives and works in Ghent (B).

Untitled, 1999.
Height: approx.
40 cm (15 ¾ in.).

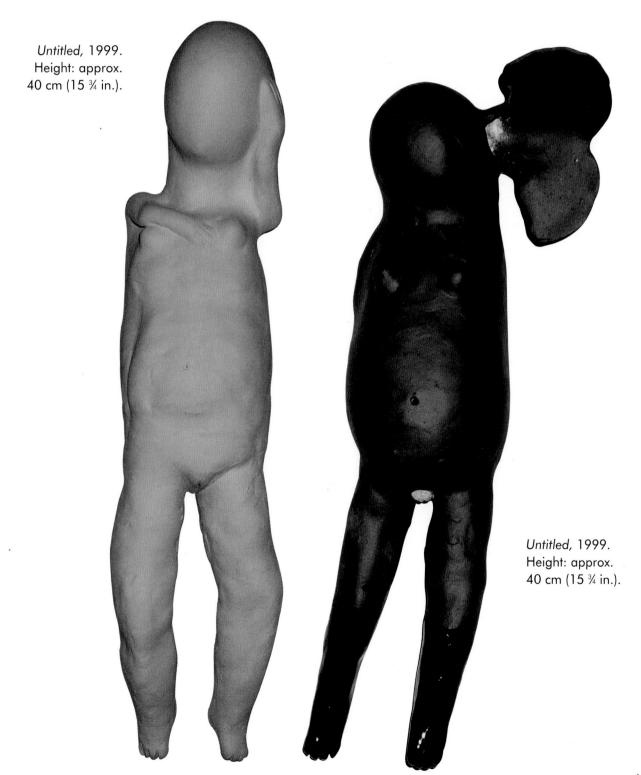

Untitled, 1999.
Height: approx.
40 cm (15 ¾ in.).

Isupov, Sergei

American. Born Stavrapole (RUS), 1963.

Studied ceramics in Tallin (EST). Moved to USA in 1993. Represented by the Ferrin Gallery in the USA; (see appendix 2). Collections include: Los Angeles County Museum (USA) (see appendix 1); Museum of Applied Art, Oslo (N). Lives and works in Richmond, Virginia (USA).

Rustle, 1999.
51 x 43 x 46 cm (20 x 17 x 18 in.).
Photographs courtesy of Ferrin Gallery.

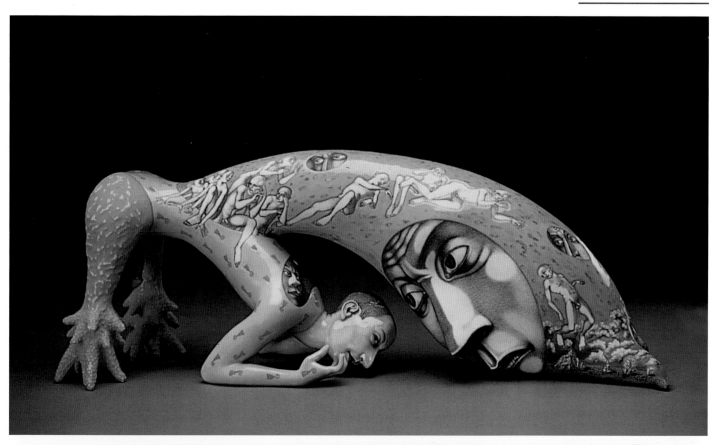

Zone, 2000.
17.75 x 47 x 15 cm (7 x 18.5 x 6 in.).
Photographs courtesy of Ferrin Gallery.

Janusonis, Audrius

Lithuanian. Born Alytus (LT), 1968.

Participates frequently in exhibitions in Lithuania, Latvia and Estonia since obtaining his diploma at Vilnius Art Academy in 1994. Collections: Panavezys Civic Gallery (LT); Latvian Artists Union Gallery (LV). Lives and works in Vilnius (LT).

RIGHT
Faun, 1999.
Red clay, enamel,
height: 55 cm (22 in.).

FAR RIGHT
Grey Mama, 1998.
Red clay, enamel, height:
60 cm (23 ½ in.).

BELOW
Shepherd, 1998.
Red clay, enamel,
height: 27 ½ in. (70 cm).

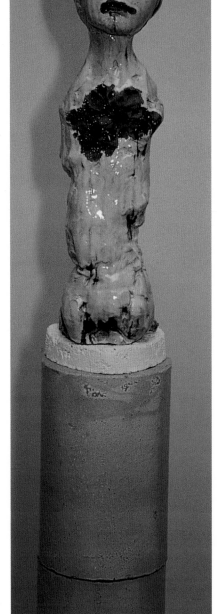

Runaway, 1998
Red clay, enamel,
height: 85 cm (33 ½ in.).

Jeanclos, Georges

French. Born Paris (F), 1933.

Trained in classical sculpture at the Ecole des Beaux Arts, Paris (F). Produced many terracotta pieces and also bronzes, several monuments and fountains in Paris and other cities. The bronze doors for the cathedral of Notre Dâme de la Treille, Lille (F) was his last major project and was completed after his death. Represented in USA by Garth Clark Gallery (see appendix 2). Collections include: Musée National d'Art Moderne, Paris (F); the Jewish Museum, New York (USA) (see appendix 1). Died Paris 1997.

Boat (Barque) For St. Julien, 1991.
Earthenware, 53 x 29 x 48 cm (21 x 11 ¼ x 19 in.).
Photograph courtesy of The Gardiner Museum, Toronto (CAN).

BELOW AND RIGHT (DETAIL)
Kamakura, 1995.
Earthenware, 30.5 x 48 x 43 cm (12 x 19 x 17 in.).
Photographs courtesy of the Garth Clark Gallery, New York.

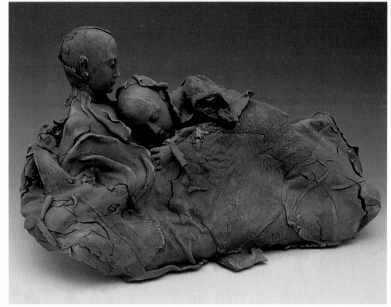

Couple (Dormeurs), 1994.
Earthenware, 25 x 47 cm (9 ¾ x 18 ½ in.).
Photograph courtesy of the Garth Clark Gallery, New York.

Head, 1983. Earthenware, 23 x 23 cm (9 x 9 in.).
Photograph courtesy of the Garth Clark Gallery, New York.

Jeck, Doug

American. Born (USA),1963.

Exhibits regularly in USA since completing MA at Chicago Art Institute in 1989. Collections include: Los Angeles County Museum (USA) (see appendix 1); International Museum of Ceramic Art at Alfred, NY (USA). Represented by Garth Clark Gallery in USA (see appendix 2). Lives and works in Seattle, Washington (USA).

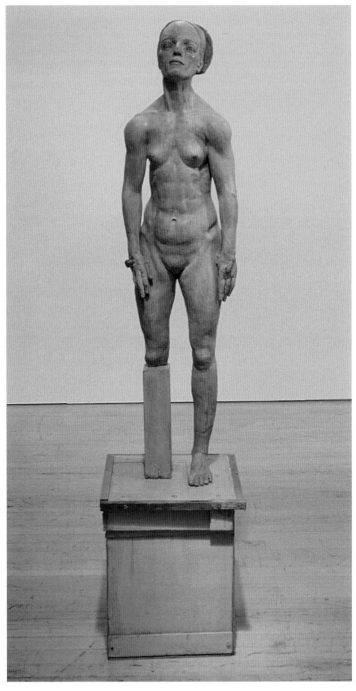

Vertical Object, 1993.
Ceramic/mixed media, 203 x 55 x 50 cm (80 x 22 x 20 in.).
Photograph courtesy Garth Clark Gallery, New York.

Du Nord, 1999.
Ceramic, wood, 170 x 41 x 46 cm (67 x 16 x 18 in.).
Photograph courtesy Garth Clark Gallery, New York.

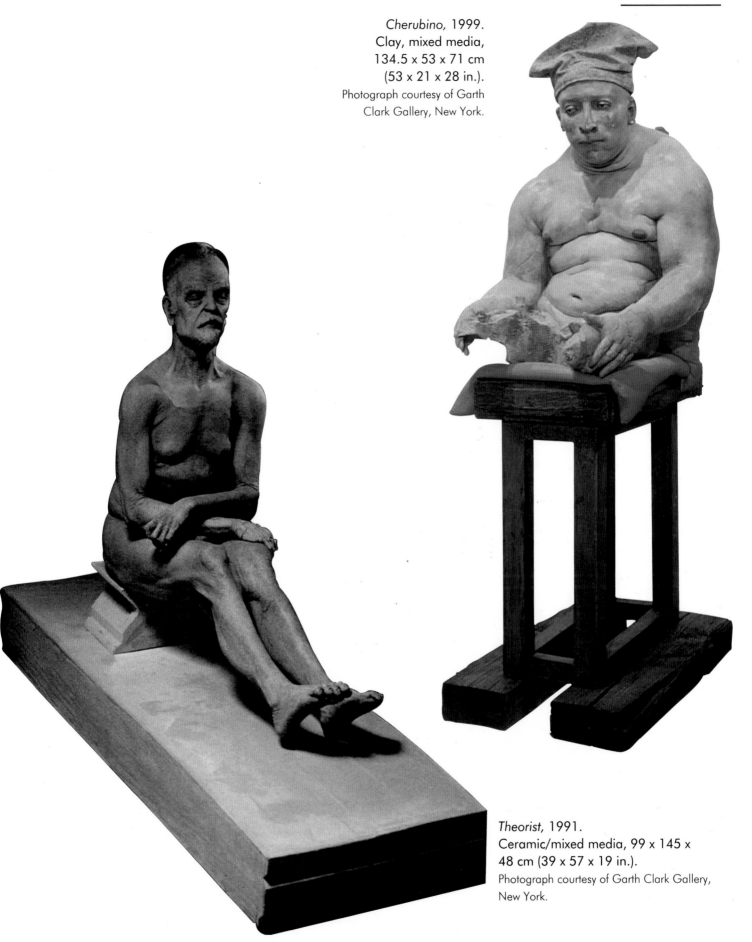

Cherubino, 1999.
Clay, mixed media,
134.5 x 53 x 71 cm
(53 x 21 x 28 in.).
Photograph courtesy of Garth
Clark Gallery, New York.

Theorist, 1991.
Ceramic/mixed media, 99 x 145 x
48 cm (39 x 57 x 19 in.).
Photograph courtesy of Garth Clark Gallery,
New York.

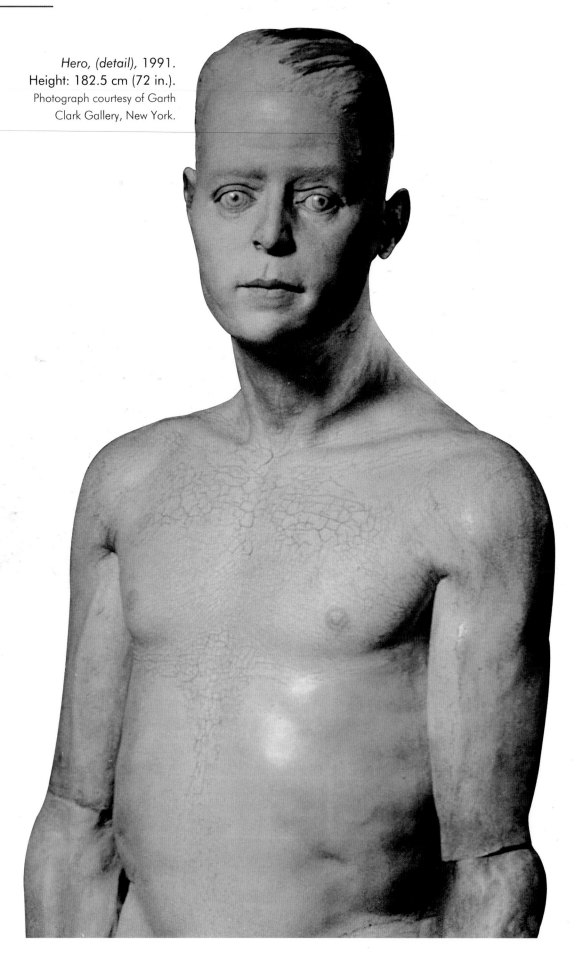

Hero, (detail), 1991.
Height: 182.5 cm (72 in.).
Photograph courtesy of Garth
Clark Gallery, New York.

Jones, Allen

British. Born Southhampton (GB),1937.

A core figure in the emergence of Pop Art in Britain in the 1960s. The piece illustrated below was made in response to a commission from Sculpture at Goodwood (GB) (see appendix 1).

Temple, 1997.
Mosaic on concrete/steel armature,
height: 800 cm (316 in.).
Photograph courtesy of Sculpture at Goodwood.

Temple, 1997.
Mosaic on concrete/steel armature,
height: 800 cm (316 in.).
Photograph courtesy of Sculpture at Goodwood.

Jupp, Mo

British. Born London (GB), 1938.

Teaches at Bristol (University of the West of England) and Harrow (University of Westminster) Schools of Art. Began working with the figure in the 1960s, often with body casts on gender-political themes. Highly active on the British ceramic scene for over 30 years. Represented by Peter's Barn (GB) (see appendix 2). Collections: Victoria and Albert Museum, London (GB); the Crafts Council of Great Britain (see appendix 1). Lives and works in London (GB).

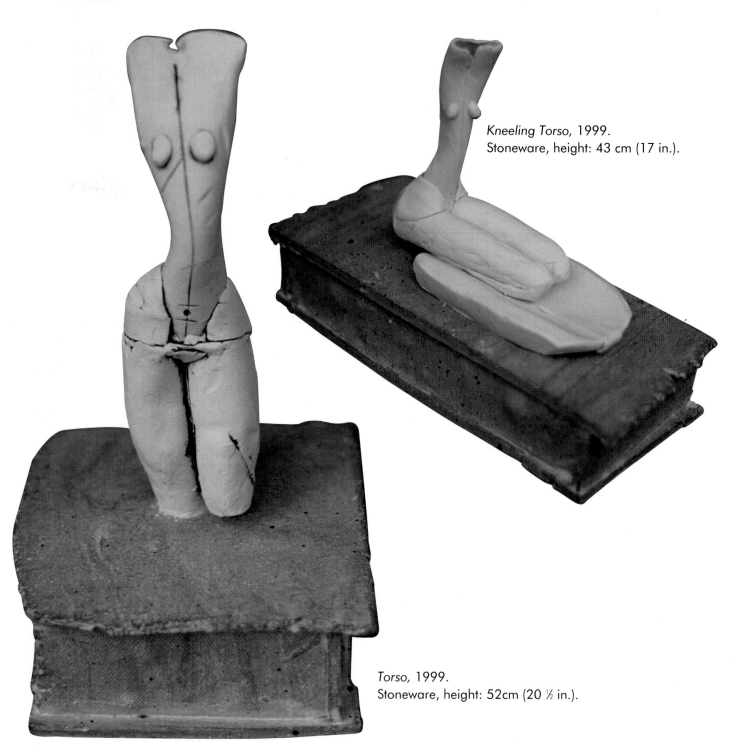

Kneeling Torso, 1999.
Stoneware, height: 43 cm (17 in.).

Torso, 1999.
Stoneware, height: 52cm (20 ½ in.).

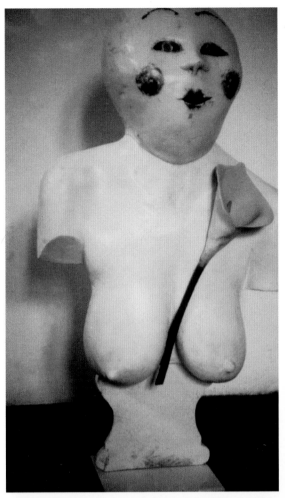

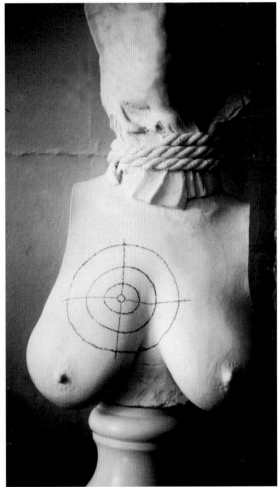

FAR LEFT
Attitude Series 1981: Doll, 1981.
Porcelain, height: 300 cm (118 ½ in.).

LEFT
Attitude Series 1981: Bag Lady, 1981.
Porcelain, height: 300 cm (118 ½ in.).

BELOW
Studio Bermondsey, London. Large sculpture: *London Lady,* 1995.
Red earthenware, high fired, 82 x 27cm (32 ½ x 10 ½ in.).

Kalkowski, Kazimiera

Polish. Born Gdansk (PL) 1954.
Collections: The National Museum, Wroclaw (PL), Museum of Porcelain, Walbbrzych (PL) (see appendix 1).
Lives and works in Gdansk (PL).

ABOVE AND RIGHT (DETAIL)
Guitar, 1996.
Porcelain, height: approx. life-size.

Coach, 1995.
Porcelain, height:
40 cm (15 ¾ in.).

Tablet 3, 1995.
Porcelain, height:
55 x 70 cm
(22 x 27 ½ in.).

Karakitsos, Kostas

Greek. Born Kavala (GR), 1956.

1984–85, apprentice to artist, Georgia Galinou, Serres (GR). Set up own studio in Kavala (GR), 1986, exhibiting regularly, mostly in Athens and Kavala since then. Lives and works in Kavala (GR).

RIGHT
African Lady, 1996.
Stoneware, height:
196 cm (77 ¼ in.).
Photograph by
Kostas Tarkassis,
courtesy of Kerameiki
Techni Magazine.

FAR RIGHT
Four Figures, 1995.
Stoneware, height:
170–220 cm
(67–86 ¾ in.).
Photograph by
Kostas Tarkassis
(courtesy of Kerameiki
Techni Magazine).

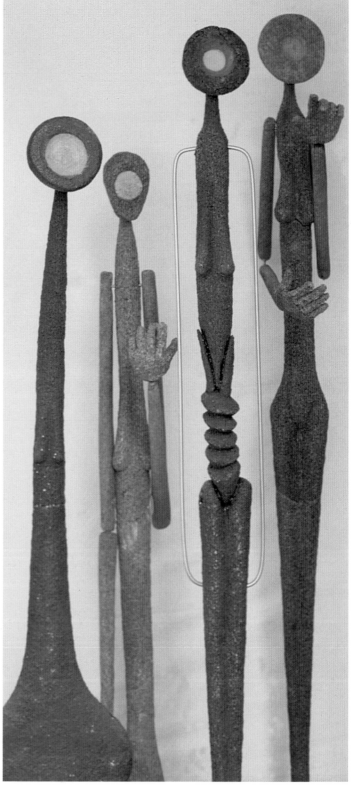

Conversation (View from Exhibition) 1998. Stoneware, height: 200 cm (79 in.). Photograph by Kostas Tarkassis (courtesy of Kerameiki Techni Magazine).

Kecskeméti, Sándor

Hungarian. Born Gyula (H), 1947.

Since 1985, Professor at the International Ceramic Studio, Kecskemét (H). Often works in stone and sometimes in bronze. Has completed many site-specific commissions around Hungary and in Germany. Member of the International Academy of Ceramics (see p.233). Collections include: Hungarian Museum of Applied Arts, Budapest (H); Museum of Applied Arts, Prague (CZ) (see appendix 1). Lives and works in Budapest (H) and in Gundremmingen (D).

The Good Shepherd, 1985.
Stoneware, height: 70 cm (27 ½ in.).
Photograph courtesy of Michael Flynn.

Sculpture, 1986.
Stoneware, height: 30 cm (11 ¾ in.).
Photograph courtesy of David Kecskeméti.

Balancing, 1991.
Stoneware, height: 120 cm (47 ¾ in.).
Photograph courtesy of Michael Flynn.

Memories of Japan, 1999.
Stoneware, height: 120 cm (47 ¾ in.).
Photograph courtesy of Michael Flynn.

Group, 1979.
Stoneware, height: 22 cm (8 ¾ in.).
Photographs courtesy of David Kecskemeti.

Keeney, Christy

Irish. Born Co. Donegal (IRL), 1958.

Since leaving Royal College of Art in 1987, has participated in a large number of exhibitions, mostly in London (GB). Several of his heads have been commissioned by prominent people, notably by HRH Prince of Wales and Sir Edward Paolozzi. Collections: Ulster Museum, Northern Ireland (GB) (see appendix 1). Lives and works in London (GB).

RIGHT
Large Round Head,
1997.
Height: 76 cm (30 in.).

FAR RIGHT
Madonna, 1999.
Height: 89 cm (35 in.).

RIGHT
Flat Head, 2000.
Height: 89 cm (35 in.).

FAR RIGHT
Trinity, 1999.
Height: 76 cm (30 in.).

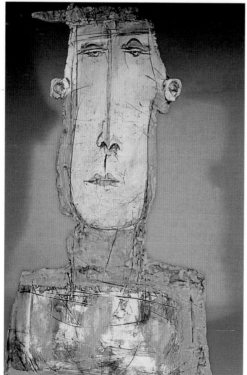

Woman with Clasped Hands, 2000. Height: 38 cm (15 in.).

Kerassioti, Maro

Greek. Born Athens (GR), 1939.

Internationally the best known Greek ceramic artist. Has published three books of poetry and one novel. Collections include: Greek Ministry of Culture, National Art Gallery of Athens (GR). Lives and works in Athens (GR).

OPPOSITE PAGE
Harpia, 1984.
Stoneware, height: 86 cm (33 ¾ in.).

Venus, 1990.
Stoneware,
height: 90 cm (35 ½ in.).

Retrospection, 1990.
Stoneware, height: 30 cm (11 ¾ in.).

Klix, Gudrun

Australian. Born Reichenbach (D), 1944.

Moved to the USA in 1950, then to Australia in 1980 after completing his MFA at University of Wisconsin (USA) in 1979. Senior lecturer, coordinator of ceramics studio, Sydney College of the Arts, University of Sydney since 1990. Collections include: Perth Art Gallery of Western Australia (see appendix 1); Museum of Applied Arts and Sciences, Sydney, NSW (AUS). Lives and works in Sydney (AUS).

Details from *Path Edge/Mind Edge*, 1984–89.
Cast ceramic, paper, soil, wood,
1067 cm (length) x 198 cm (highest point), (420 x 78 in.).

Red Dish, 1997.
Terracotta with copper oxide, 76 x 16 x 10 cm (30 x 6 ¼ x 4 in.).

LEFT
Erdknator, 1994.
79 x 37.5 x 19 cm
(31 x 14 ¾ x 7 ½ in.).

Untitled, 1994.
Earthenware, oxides, glaze,
length: 50 cm (20 in.).

Kottler, Howard

American. Born Cleveland, Ohio (USA), 1930.

In 1957 worked at Arabia Factory (FIN). 1965-1989, Professor, University of Washington, Seattle (USA). Prolific maker of striking and highly innovative work. 'One of the most influential teachers in the ceramic sculpture movement' (Garth Clark). 'An influential and powerful force shaping and defining the "look" of contemporary American ceramic sculpture' (Judith S. Schwartz). Collections include: American Craft Museum, New York, (USA)(see appendix 1); National Museum of Modern Art, Kyoto (JAP). Died Seattle 1989.

Slim, 1989.
Glazed earthenware,
73.5 x 38 x 19 cm
(29 x 15 x 7.5 in.).
Photograph courtesy of
Roger Schreiber.

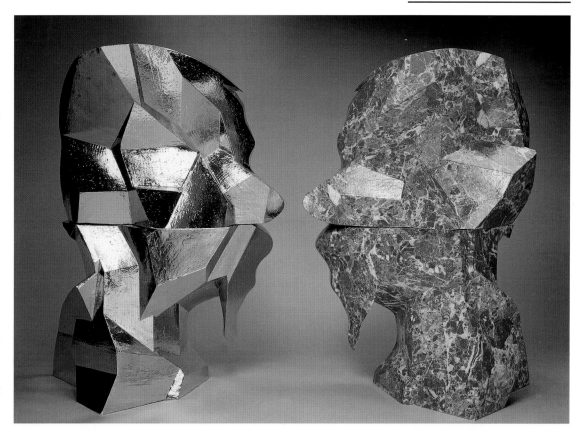

Double Identity, 1985.
Ceramic with decals,
100 x 71 x 40.5 cm
(39 ½ x 28 x 16 in.).
Photograph courtesy of
Roger Schreiber.

BELOW
Double Identity,
(back view), 1985.
Photograph courtesy of
Roger Schreiber.

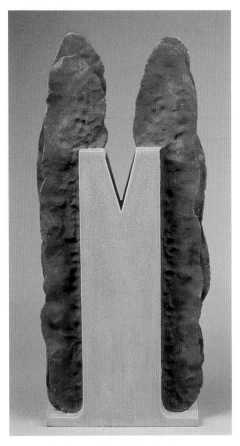

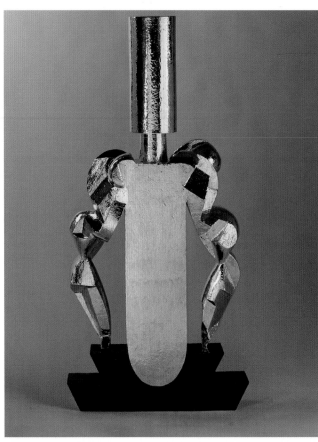

FAR LEFT
Big Romaine Pot, 1987.
Earthenware, glazes,
73.5 x 29 x 10 cm
(29 x 11 ½ x 4 in.).

LEFT
Posing as a Cubist,
1987.
Earthenware, glaze
and lustre,
86 x 43 x 12.75 cm
(34 x 17 x 5 in.).
Photograph by Roger
Schreiber.

BELOW
Tongue Twister, 1986.
Ceramic and mixed
media,
185.5 x 228.5 x 146 cm
(73 x 90 x 24 in.).

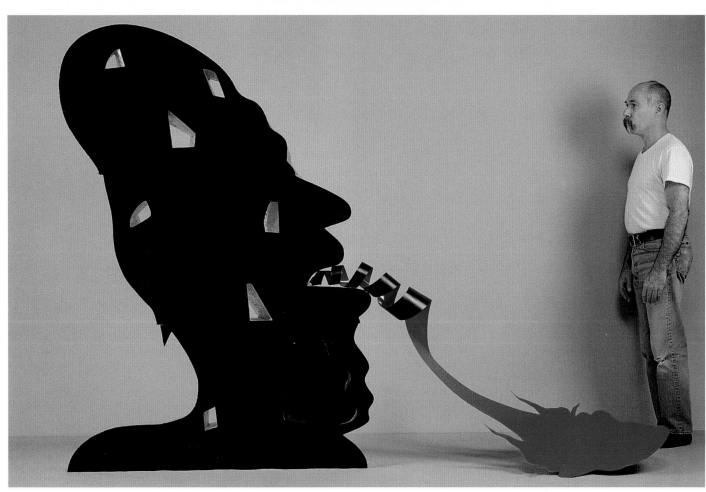

Kuczyńska, Maria Teresa

Polish. Born Elblag (PL), 1948.

Internationally the best known Polish clay artist. Also works in bronze, including site-specific commissions in Australia. Member of the International Academy of Ceramics (see p.233). Collections include: The National Museum, Wroclaw (PL); International Ceramic Museum, Faenza (I) (see appendix 1). Lives and works in Sopot (PL).

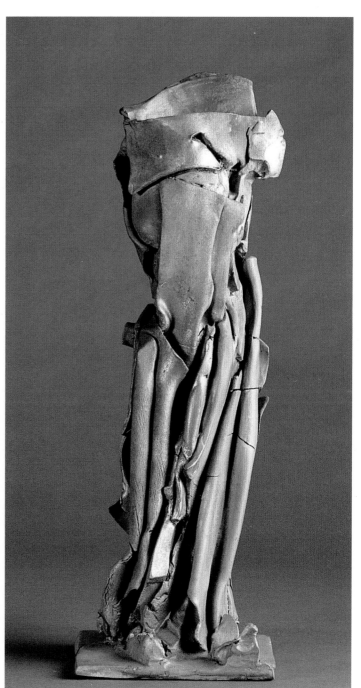

Green Torso, 1997.
Stoneware and glaze, 54 x 19 x 19 cm
(21 ¼ x 7 ½ x 7 ½ in.).

Grey Column, 1997.
Shigaraki black clay,
height: 53 cm (21 in.).

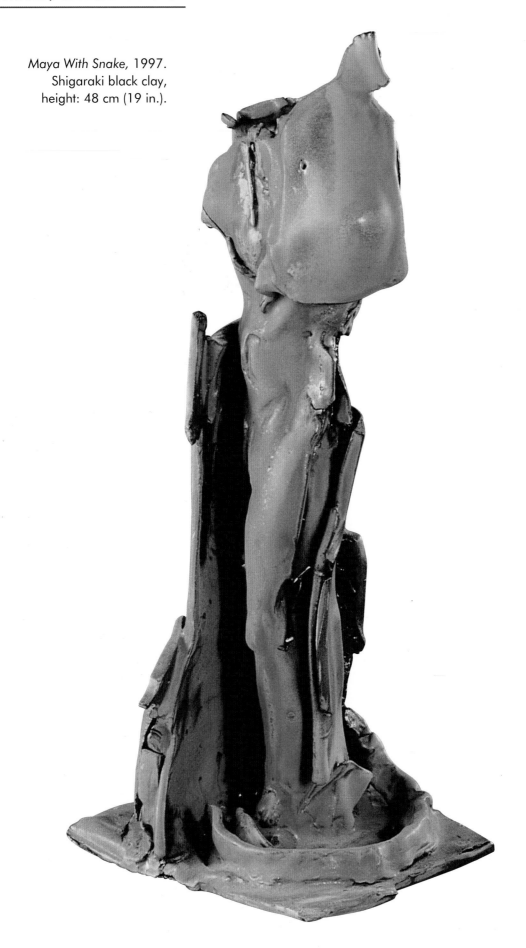

Maya With Snake, 1997.
Shigaraki black clay,
height: 48 cm (19 in.).

Kvasyte, Jolante

Lithuanian. Born Vilnius (LT), 1956.

Well-known internationally, having exhibited widely in Europe and the USA. Collections include: The National Museum, Wroclaw (PL) (see appendix 1); National Gallery of Applied Arts, Vilnius (LT). Lives and works in Vilnius (LT).

ABOVE LEFT
Salomea, 1999.
Clay, glaze and enamel, height: 35 cm (13 ¾ in.).

ABOVE
Dancer on the Stick, 1999.
Clay, glaze and enamel, height: 36 cm (14 ¼ in.).

LEFT
Comet, (detail) 1998.
Red clay, enamel, height (tallest): 120 cm (47 ¾ in.).

Lucero, Michael

American. Born Tracy, California (USA), 1953.

Highly popular in the USA. Huge output of work. Has many awards including the National Endowment for Arts Fellowship and the Richard Koopman Distinguished Chair for the Arts, University of Hartford. Collections include: the Hirschhorn Museum and Sculpture Garden, Washington, DC (USA); the Metropolitan Museum of Art, New York (USA) (see appendix 1). Lives and works in Upper Nyack, New York (USA).

Southwest Dreamer, 1984.
Glazed ceramic, 51 x 67 x 63 cm (20 x 26 x 25 in.).
Photograph courtesy of Franklin Parrasch Gallery, New York.

Anthropomorphic Baby Form in Red Stroller, 1994 (*New World Series*). Clay with glazes, metal stroller. Approx: 66 x 40.5 x 71cm (26 x 16 x 28 in.). Photograph courtesy of Franklin Parrasch Gallery, New York.

FAR RIGHT AND
RIGHT (DETAIL)
Model, 1997.
Clay with glazes,
wood and metal stand,
205.75 x 58 x 56 cm
(81 x 23 x 22 in.).
Photograph courtesy of
Franklin Parrasch
Gallery, New York.

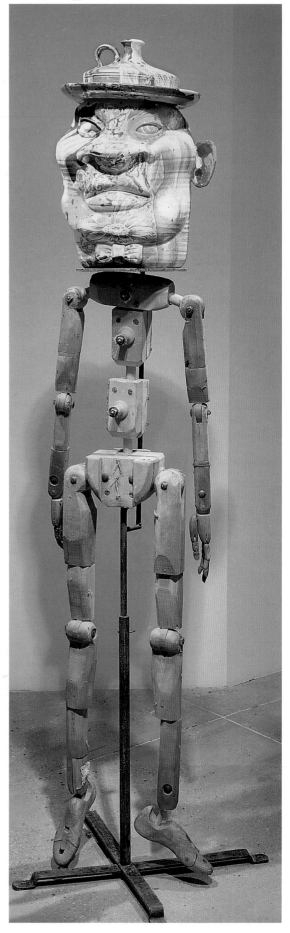

RIGHT
Modest Lady, 1996,
(*Reclamation Series*).
Clay with glazes, plaster,
94 x 25.5 x 25.5 cm
(37 x 10 x 10 in.).
Photograph courtesy of
Franklin Parrasch
Gallery, New York.

MacDonnell, Sally

British. Born Boston, Lincolnshire (GB), 1971.

Exhibits regularly since leaving Bath Spa University in 1997. Recently produced installation work can be seen at McHardy Sculpture Company, London (GB). Collections: Egner Collection, Frechen (D) (see appendix 1). Lives and works in Bath (GB).

LEFT
Reclining Figure, 1997. Smoked ceramic and pewter, 31 x 16 x 33cm (12 x 6 ¼ x 13 in.). Photograph by Peter Reynolds.

FAR LEFT
Standing Figure, 1999. Smoked ceramic and pewter, height: 58 cm (22 ¾ in.). Photograph by Peter Reynolds.

Torso, 1999. Smoked ceramic, height: 32 cm (12 ½ in.).

Seated Figures, 1997. Smoked porcelain, pewter and steel, height: 32–34 cm (12½ –14 ¼ in.).

Mákelá, Maarit

Finnish. Born Helsinki (FIN), 1961.

Teaches at the University of Art and Design, Helsinki (FIN). Completed MA at the same university in 1995. From 1992–93 studied painting at the National College of Art and Design, Dublin (IRL). Collections: State of Finland Collection, Helsinki (FIN); Sodankylä County, Lapland (FIN) and the Helander Foundation (FIN). Lives and works in Helsinki (FIN).

Speculum II, 1997 (Kermische Installation).
Ceramic with silkscreen print, 120 x 65 cm
(47 ¾ x 25 ½ in.).
Photograph by Rauno Traskelin.

Speculum II, (detail), 1997
(Kermische Installation).
Ceramic with silkscreen print,
120 x 65 cm (47 ¾ x 25 ½ in.).
Photograph by Rauno Traskelin.

*Verwirrung Wieder and
Wieder*, 1996.
Ceramic collage,
75 x 21 cm
(29 ½ x 8 ¼ in.).
Photograph by
Rauno Traskelin.

Mitchell, Craig

British. Born Irvine, Scotland (GB), 1967.

Completed MA at the Royal College of Art, London (GB) in 1992. Since then has exhibited regularly in Scotland and at Contemporary Applied Arts, London (see appendix 2). Collections: the Royal Museum of Scotland, Edinburgh (GB); Yingko County Museum, Taipei (TW). Lives and works in Edinburgh, Scotland (GB).

ABOVE
Thoroughly Modern Mother, 1998.
Glazed ceramic,
height: 47 cm (18 ½ in.).

Stormy Seas for the French Fancymen, 1998.
Glazed ceramic,
height: 61 cm (24 in.).

Roller Coaster Emotions, 1997. Glazed ceramic, height: 160 cm (63 in.).

Möhwald, Gertraud

German. Born Dresden (D), 1929.

Highly respected and influential figure in Germany. Originally studied stone sculpture at the Dresden Zwinger, 1948-50. Member of the International Academy of Ceramics (see p.233). Collections include: Keramikmuseum, Westerwald (D) (see appendix 1); State Art Collection, Dresden (D). Lives and works in Halle (D) and in Berlin (D).

Large Bust in Five Parts, 1996.
Grogged clay with porcelain shards, 180 x 83 x 170 cm
(71 x 32 ½ x 67 in.).
Photograph by Bernd Kuhnert, Berlin.

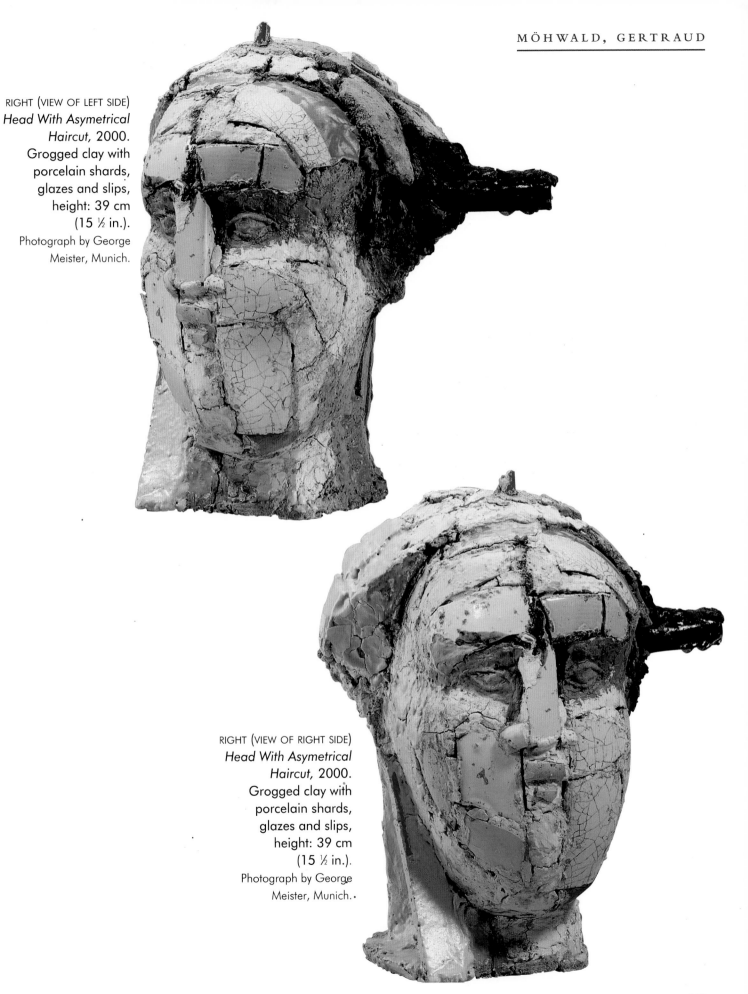

RIGHT (VIEW OF LEFT SIDE)
*Head With Asymetrical
Haircut*, 2000.
Grogged clay with
porcelain shards,
glazes and slips,
height: 39 cm
(15 ½ in.).
Photograph by George
Meister, Munich.

RIGHT (VIEW OF RIGHT SIDE)
*Head With Asymetrical
Haircut*, 2000.
Grogged clay with
porcelain shards,
glazes and slips,
height: 39 cm
(15 ½ in.).
Photograph by George
Meister, Munich.

Möhwald, Gertraud

RIGHT

Torso with Bowed Head, 1984.
Grogged earthenware with porcelain shards and glazes, height: 65 cm (25 ½ in.).
Photograph by Marcus Nawlik, Halle.

FAR RIGHT

Head of L.M., 1991.
Grogged earthenware with porcelain shards and glazes, height: 37 cm (14 ½ in.).
Photograph by George Meister, courtesy of Gallery B15, Munich.

BELOW

Bust of Old Woman with Raised Hand, 1993.
Grogged earthenware with porcelain shards and glazes, height: 52 cm (20 ¾ in.).
Photograph by Klaus Eberhardgöltz, Halle, courtesy of Gallery B15.

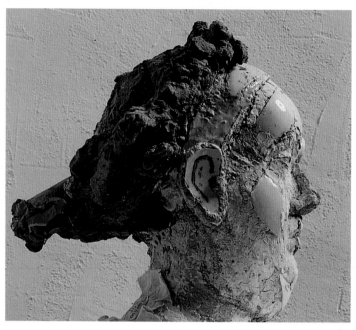

BELOW

Right Hand.
Grogged earthenware with porcelain shards and glazes, height: 45 cm (17 ¾ in.).
Photograph by Klaus Eberhardgöltz, Halle, courtesy of Gallery B15.

Moonellis, Judy

American. Born Jackson Heights, Queens, New York (USA), 1953.

Actively exhibiting and teaching widely in USA since completing MFA at Alfred University (USA) in 1978. Collections include: American Craft Museum, New York (USA); Renwick Gallery, Smithsonian Institution, Washington, (USA) (see appendix 1). Lives and works in New York City (USA).

Memory Portraits: Hands, 1996–98.
Clay, encaustic, steel, 38 x 122 x 20 cm (15 x 48 x 8 in.).

New Parts, 1995.
114.5 x 71 x 12.5 cm
(45 x 28 x 5 in.).

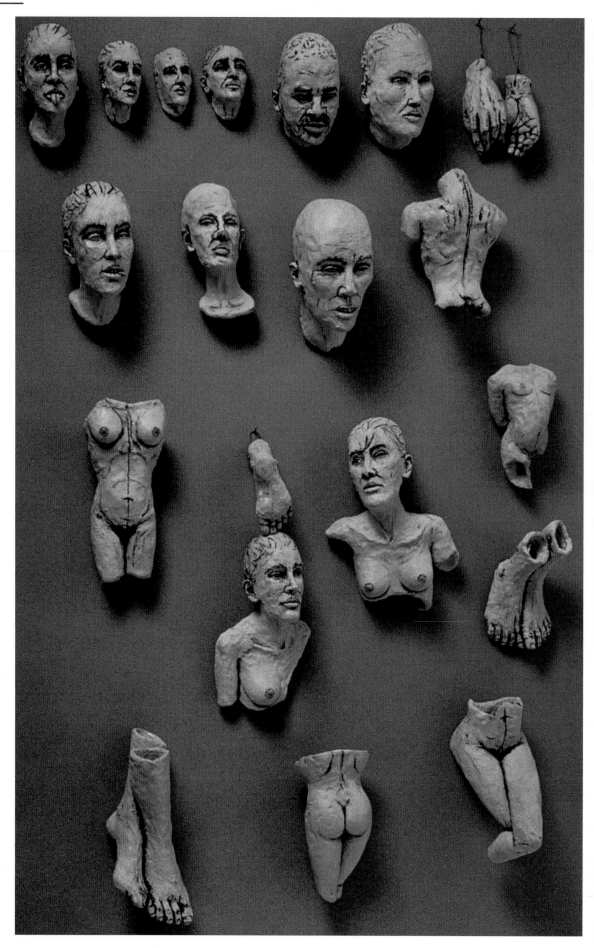

LEFT AND BELOW LEFT (DETAIL),
Wheels, 1996–98.
Mixed Media, 190 x 53 x 244 cm (75 x 21 x 96 in.).

BELOW
Sweet Element, 1998.
Clay, copper, iron, rock, sugar, 12.7 x 38 x 38 cm (5 x 15 x 15 in.).

BOTTOM
Bare, 1998.
Clay, plaster, encaustic, 25.5 x 20 x 12.7 cm (10 x 8 x 5 in.).

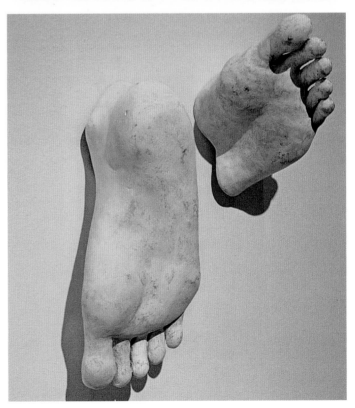

Muys, Hermann

Belgian. Born Saint-Amand (Puurs) (B), 1944.

Studied at the Royal Academy of Fine Arts and the National School of Fine Arts, both in Antwerp (B), 1961-68. Exhibiting his ceramic sculptures regularly in Belgium since 1979. Completed a number of monumental murals for various government buildings in Belgium. Collections include: Rockefeller Art Centre, State University of New York (USA); Provinciehuis, Antwerp (B). Lives and works in Ghent (B).

Green, 1994.
Height (figure only): 52 cm (20 ½ in.).

Paper Hat, 1999.
Height: 70 cm (27 ½ in.).

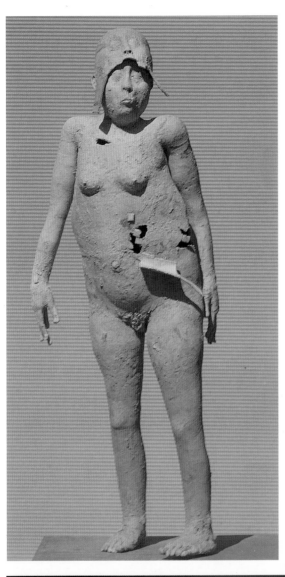

Nadleman, Elie

American. Born Warsaw, Polish Russia, 1882.

Emigrated to USA 1914. Worked in plaster, bronze and papier maché. Began experimenting with ceramics between 1930–35 with the aim of producing large editions of small sculpture. Thereafter worked mostly in plastiline (an oil-based material) having had to sell his studio and kiln. Died New York City 1946.

RIGHT
Two Women, undated.
Glazed decorated ceramic,
43 x 25.5 x 15 cm
(17 x 10 x 6 in.).
Photograph courtesy of Salander O' Reilly Gallery, New York.

FAR RIGHT
Two Women,
c. mid 1930–46.
Glazed decorated ceramic,
41.5 x 20 x 15 cm
(16 ¼ x 9 x 6 in.).
Photograph courtesy of Salander O' Reilly Gallery, New York.

RIGHT
Seated Women,
c. mid 1930–46.
17 x 14.5 x 14 cm
(6 ¾ x 5 ¾ x 5 ½ in.).
Photograph courtesy of Salander O' Reilly Gallery, New York.

FAR RIGHT
Woman with Poodle,
c.1935–6.
Earthenware.
19 x 14 cm
(7 ½ x 5 ½ in.).
Photograph courtesy of Salander O' Reilly Gallery, New York.

Neubert, Martin

German. Born Kleinmachnow near Berlin (D), 1965.

Also works in stone and in concrete. Collections include: Museum of Applied Arts, Gera (D); Marburg University Museum of Art and Cultural History, Marburg (D). Lives and works in Taupadel near Bürgel, Thuringia (D).

Fall, 1996.
Ceramic, acrylic, concrete, 250 x 250 cm (98 ½ x 98 ½ in.).

Head, 1996.
Wood fired with slips,
height: 52 cm (20 ½ in.).
Photograph by Guntard Linde.

Dancer, 1994.
Wood fired with slips
and glazes, height:
68 cm (26 ¼ in.).

Reclining Torso, 1994.
Assembled ceramic slabs, concrete, steel.
50 x 170 x 70 cm (20 x 67 x 27 ½ in.).
Photograph by Guntard Linde.

Novak, Justin

American. Born Kansas City, Missouri (USA), 1962.

1983–93 worked as illustrator for, among others *The New York Times*, Harper & Row and Macmillans. Completed MFA at State University of New York, Palz, in 1996. Presently teaching in the art department, University of Oregon, Eugene (USA). Collections: Mint Museum, North Carolina (USA); Everson Museum of Art, Syracuse, New York (USA) (see appendix 1). Lives and works in Eugene, Oregon (USA).

LEFT AND BELOW (DETAIL)
Disfigurine , 1996.
Raku fired ceramic, 33 x 12.5 x
12.5 cm (13 x 5 x 5 in.).

Provider, 1996.
Raku fired ceramic,
41 x 18 x 18 cm
(16 x 7 x 7 in.).

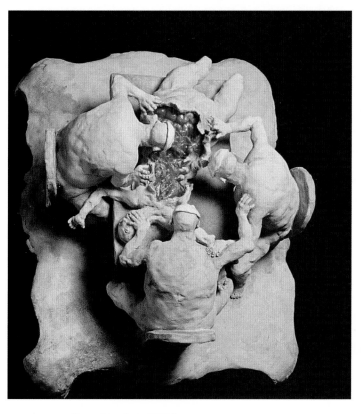

Free Market, 1996.
28 x 50 x 41 cm (11 x 20 x 16 in.).

Free Market, 1996.
28 x 50 x 41 cm (11 x 20 x 16 in.).

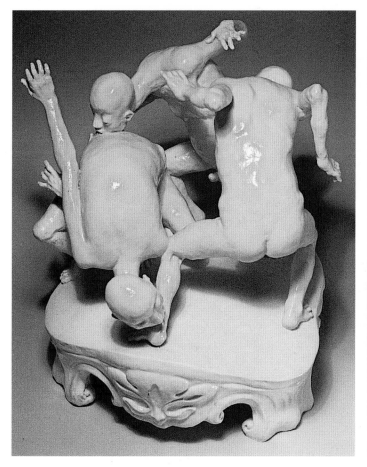

Disfigurine, 1999.
38 x 30.5 x 30.5 cm (15 x 12 x 12 in.).

Disfigurine, 1999.
38 x 30.5 x 30.5 cm (15 x 12 x 12 in.).

Oka Doner, Michelle

American. Born Miami Beach, Florida (USA), 1943.

Highly active in the American ceramic scene during the late 1960s, 1970s and 1980s. Has concentrated on large scale public art projects during the last ten years. Often incorporating embedded cast bronze artifacts, notably the half-mile long floor of Miami International Airport (USA). Collections include: Art Institute of Chicago, Illinois (USA); Virginia Museum of Fine Arts, Richmond, Virginia (USA) (see appendix 1). Lives and works in New York City (USA).

Untitled, 1973.
Porcelain and earthenware, height (left figure): 51 cm (20 ½ in.), (right figure): 54 cm (21 ¼ in.).
Photograph courtesy of Garth Clark Gallery, New York.

Figures with Staffs,
1984–7.
Porcelain and
earthenware. Height:
54 cm (21 ¼ in.).
Photograph by
Dirk Bakker.

Burial Pieces, 1975.
Size of pelvis:
35.5 x 57.5 x 53 cm
(14 x 23 x 21 in.).

159

Figure with Staff, 1985.
Earthenware and poreclain,
height (figure): 43 cm (17 in.),
(staff): 50 cm (20 in.).

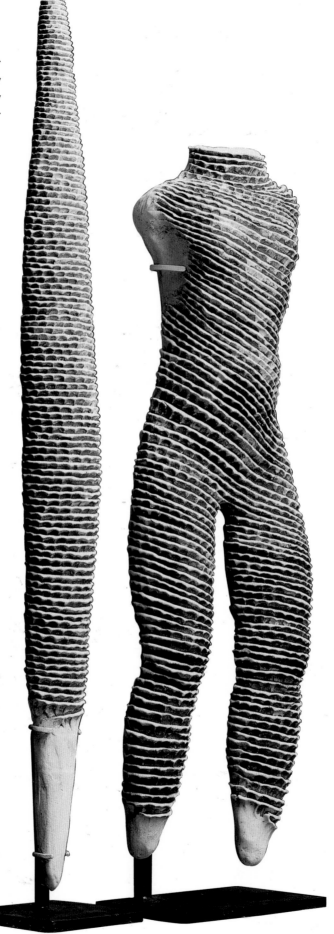

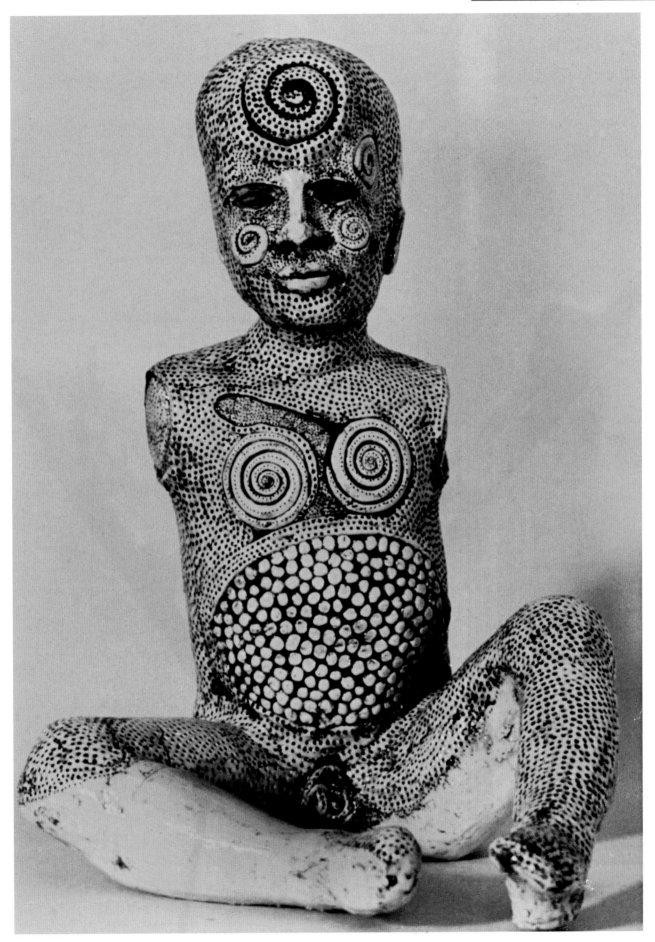

Onnen, Sybille

German. Born Obendorf-Neckar (D), 1944.

Teaches at the State Kunsthalle, Karlsruhe (D) (since 1985) and the Karlsruhe College of Education (since 1989). Frequent exhibitions, mostly in Karlsruhe and Baden–Württemberg (D), since 1980. Collections include: Karlsruhe City Collection (D); Nord-Baden Governing Council (D). Lives and works in Karlsruhe (D) and in Keffernach, Alsace (F).

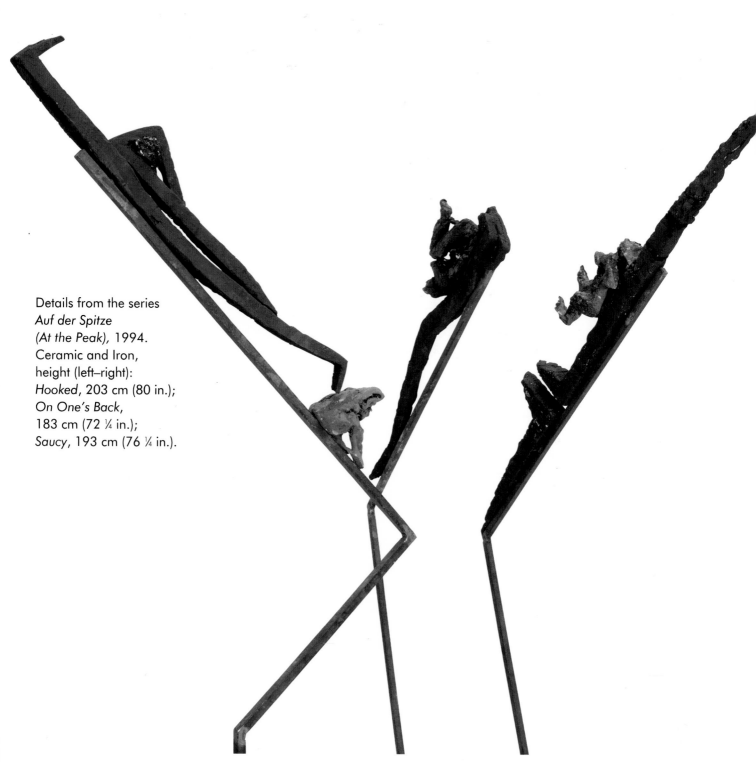

Details from the series
Auf der Spitze
(At the Peak), 1994.
Ceramic and Iron,
height (left–right):
Hooked, 203 cm (80 in.);
On One's Back,
183 cm (72 ¼ in.);
Saucy, 193 cm (76 ¼ in.).

At the Peak, 1994.
Ceramic and Iron, height:
203 cm (80 in.).

TOP
Figures, 1989.
Height (tallest): 24 cm (9 ½ in.).
Photograph by Irmtrud Saarbourg.

BOTTOM
Pair, 1990.
Ceramic with slip, height: 18 cm (7 in.).
Photograph by Irmtrud Saarbourg.

Paral, Miroslav

Czech. Born Prague (CZ), 1955.

Founder of the International Clay Studio, Česky Krumlov. Has completed several large-scale architectural works in Česky Krumlov and Česky Budejovice. Collections include: Agency for Czech Design, Česky Krumlov (CZ); International Ceramics Museum, Kecskemét (H) (see appendix 1). Lives and works in Česky Krumlov (CZ).

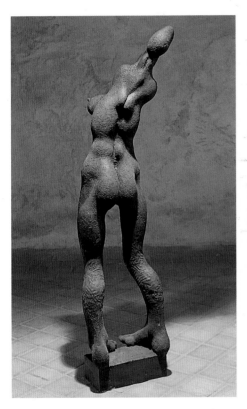  

ABOVE (LEFT AND FAR RIGHT)
Figures, 1996.
Stoneware, height:
up to 195 cm (77 in.).

CENTRE (ABOVE AND BELOW)
Aggression of Time II, 1997.
Stoneware, clay and metal,
height: 85 cm (33 ½ in.).

165

RIGHT
Aggression (Libido, Ego).1991.
Stoneware, clay
and metal, height:
178 cm (70 ¼ in.).

OPPOSITE PAGE
Atlases (situated in
Česky-Budojevice),
1994.
Stoneware, height:
320 cm (125 ½ in.).

Pauwels, Achiel

Belgian. Born Ghent (B), 1932.

Professor, Royal Academy of Fine Art, Antwerp (B), 1965-92. Has been exhibiting, mostly in Belgium and Holland since 1952. Several site-specific commissions, mostly in Flanders (B). Collections include: National Museum of Wales, Cardiff (GB) (see appendix 1); National Museum for Art and Culture, Brussels (B). Lives and works in Ghent (B).

The Table of Babel, 1981.
Stoneware, life-size figures.

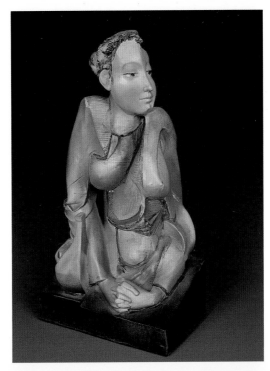

RIGHT
Portrait – Irene, 1990.
Porcelain, height:
50 cm (20 in.).

BELOW
Sarajevo, 1993.
Coloured slips on
earthenware, life-size figures.

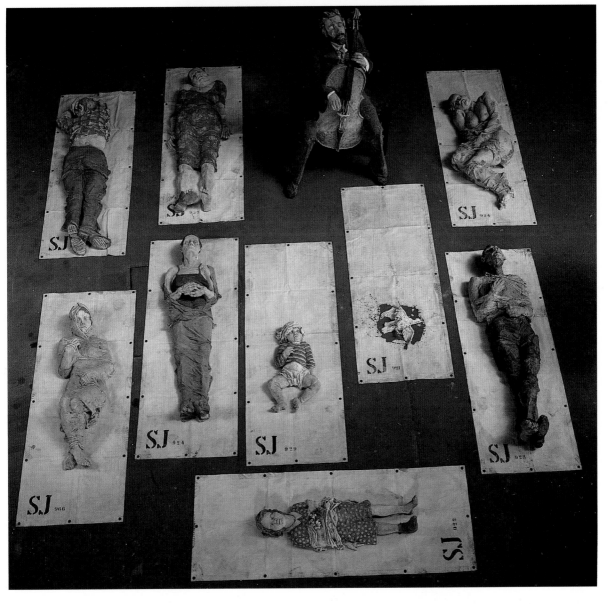

Payce, Greg

Canadian. Born Edmonton, Alberta (CAN), 1956.

Senior Lecturer, Alberta College of Art and Design, Calgary (CAN), since 1988. Exhibiting regularly throughout Canada since completing MFA at Nova Scotia College of Art and Design in 1987. Member of the International Academy of Ceramics (see p.233). Collections include: the Canadian Clay and Glass Gallery, Waterloo, Ontario (CAN) (see appendix 1); The Royal Ontario Museum, Toronto (CAN). Represented by Prime Gallery; Toronto (CAN); Nancy Margolis Gallery, New York (USA) (see appendix 2). Lives and works in Calgary, Alberta (CAN).

Freeze, (detail), 1996.
Earthenware. 240 x 18 x 21cm (94 ½ x 7 x 8 ¼ in.).

TOP
Apparently, 1999.
Earthenware. 102 x 30 x 92cm
(40 ¼ x 11 ¾ x 36 ¼ in.).

BOTTOM
Morph, 1998.
Earthenware. 76 x 18 x 27cm
(30 x 7 x 10 ½ in).

Peascod, Alan

Australian. Born Workington, Cumbria (GB), 1943.

Head of Ceramics, Illiwarra Institute of Technology, 1986–98. A leading figure in Australian ceramics for many years through teaching and research as well as practice. Also produces a wide range of vessel forms. Completed Doctorate in Creative Arts, University of Wollogong, 1994. Collections include: Australian National Art Gallery, Canberra (AUS); Alhambra Museum Collection, Granada (E). Lives and works in Gulgong, New South Wales, (AUS).

ABOVE
Silent Scream, 1998.
Vitreous terracotta, height: 20 cm (8 in.).

OPPOSITE PAGE
Figure, (detail) 1997.
Vitreous porcelain, height: 37 cm (14 ½ in.).

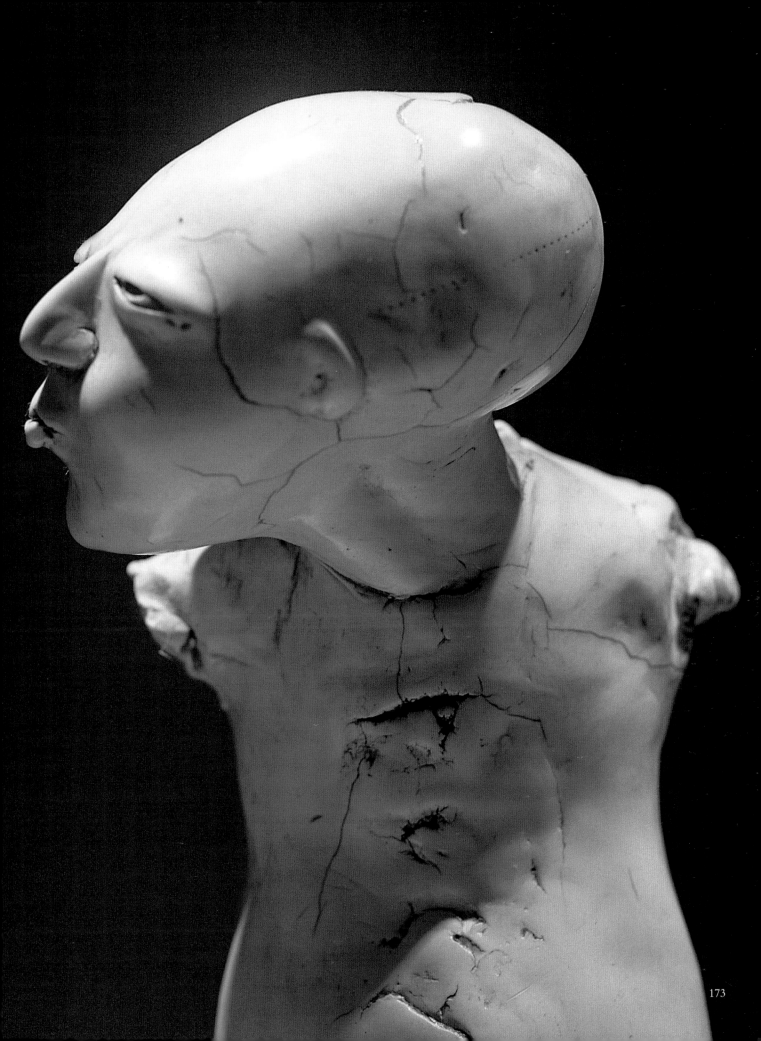

RIGHT
Street Kid Series: Matthew, 1997.
Vitreous porcelain, height: 35 cm (13 ¾ in.).

FAR RIGHT (DETAIL)
Fence Sitter, 1997.
Vitreous porcelain, height: 38 cm (15 in.).

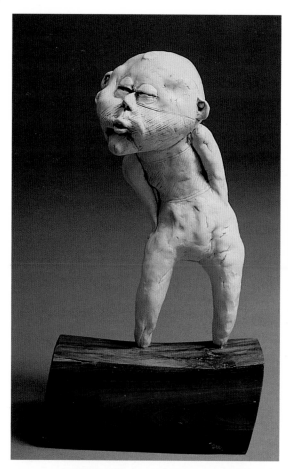

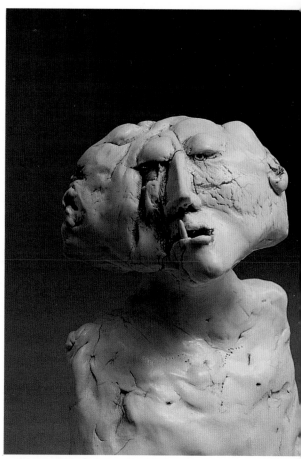

RIGHT
Sceptics Society: Figure with Crushed Tinnie, 1998.
Vitreous porcelain, height: 35 cm (13 ¾ in.).

FAR RIGHT
Dead Fish Society, 1996.
Vitreous porcelain, height: 80 cm (31 ½ in.).

Perrigo, Anne

American. Born Newfoundland (CAN), 1953.

1995–99, Assistant Professor, University of Texas, El Paso (USA). Has exhibited widely in USA since completing MA at University of California, Davis in 1978. Collections: included in slide packet, *Political Ceramics*, published by American Craft Museum, New York (USA); Seattle City Light Portable Works Collection (USA). Lives and works in Seattle, Washington (USA).

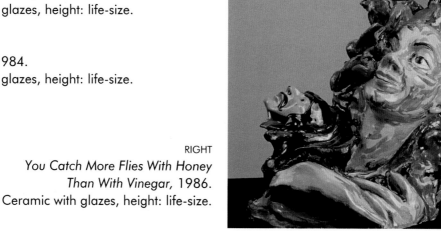

ABOVE
Magnetic Attraction, 1985.
Ceramic with glazes, height: life-size.

ABOVE RIGHT
Dreamboat, 1984.
Ceramic with glazes, height: life-size.

RIGHT
*You Catch More Flies With Honey
Than With Vinegar*, 1986.
Ceramic with glazes, height: life-size.

RIGHT
Orbit, 1991.
Ceramic with glazes,
height: life-size.

FAR RIGHT
Diana and Acteon:
Blinded by the Light,
1993.
Ceramic with glazes,
height: life-size.

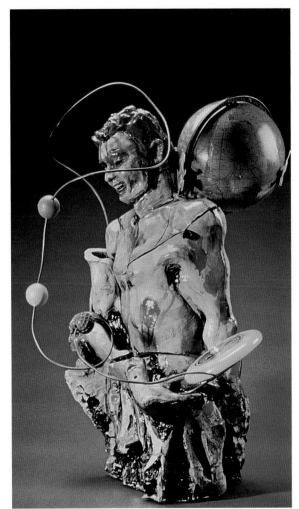

RIGHT
Jane Doe, 1999.
Clay, wood, plastic,
taxidermy form,
height: life-size.

OPPOSITE PAGE
Diana and Acteon:
Blinded by the Light,
(detail) 1993.
Ceramic with glazes,
height: life-size.

Purkrábková, Hana

Czech. Born Tábor (CZ), 1936.

Prominent figure in Czech ceramics for nearly 30 years. Collections include: Museum of Applied Arts, Prague (CZ) (see appendix 1), the Clay Studio, Philadelphia (USA). Lives and works in Prague (CZ).

ABOVE (DETAIL) AND RIGHT
At the Table, 1995.
16 x 16 cm
(6 ¼ x 6 ¼ in.).

OPPOSITE PAGE
Two Women, 1997.
Approx: life-size.

Schmidt-Reuther, Gisela

German. Born Sobernheim, Nahe (D), 1915.

Active ceramic artist for over 60 years, having studied ceramics at the State School for Ceramics, Höhr Greuzhausen (D), from 1934–36. Later worked at the Karlsruhe Maiolica Factory 1937-40 as well as studying sculpture at schools in Frankfurt, Berlin and Trier, 1936–45. Associate of Georg Kolbe 1940–44. Continues to work in her studio in Rengsdorf (D) since 1952. Member of the International Academy of Ceramics (see p.233). Collections include: Hetjens Museum, Düsseldorf (D); Taipei Fine Arts Museum (TW) (see appendix 1). Several site-specific commissions.

Antlitz, 1984.
Stoneware with
barium glaze,
18 x 16 x 2 cm
(7 x 6 ¼ x ¾ in.).

ABOVE LEFT
Theater Pause, 1980.
Stoneware,
45 x 30 x 8 cm
(17 ¾ x 11 ¾ x 3 in.).

ABOVE RIGHT
Halbakt, 1967.
Stoneware, height:
40 cm (15 ¾ in.).

LEFT
Zuwendung, 1985.
Stoneware,
40 x 45 x 18 cm
(15 ¾ x 17 ¾ x 7 in.).

Schrammel, Imre

Hungarian. Born Szombathely (H), 1933.

The first modern ceramic artist in Hungary, having produced a wide range of experimental work. His influence on successive generations of Hungarian artists is enormous. 1993-2000, Rector of the Hungarian Academy of Applied Arts, Budapest (H). Exhibits throughout Europe. Member of the International Academy of Ceramics (see p.233). Collections include: Museum of Applied Arts, Budapest (H); Victoria and Albert Museum, London (GB) (see appendix 1). Lives and works in Budapest (H).

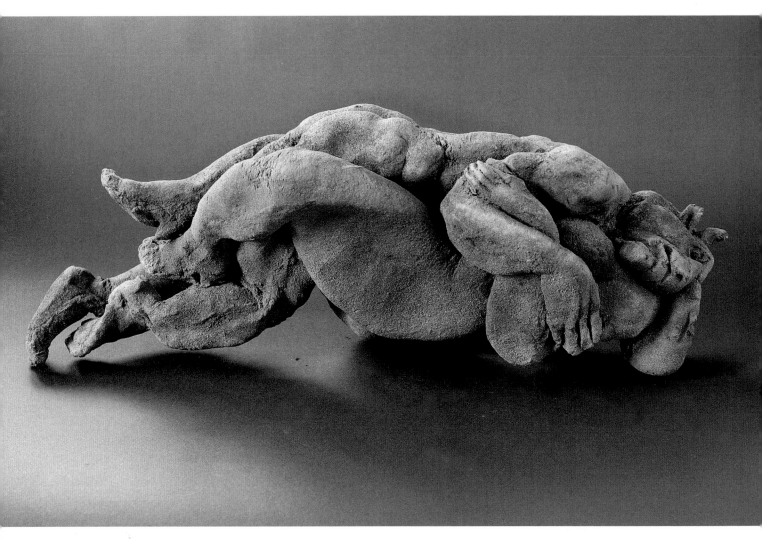

Liebe, 1986.
Stoneware, 17 x 52 x 19 cm (6 ¾ x 20 ½ x 7 ½ in.) .

Karneval, 1997.
Porcelain,
36 cm (14 ¼ in.).

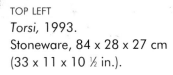

TOP LEFT
Torsi, 1993.
Stoneware, 84 x 28 x 27 cm
(33 x 11 x 10 ½ in.).

TOP RIGHT
Minotaur With Girl, 1988.
Stoneware, 44 x 30 x 23 cm
(17 ½ x 11 ¾ x 9 in.).

BOTTOM LEFT
Prone Figure, 1993.
Stoneware, 79 x 38 x 27 cm
(31 ¼ x 15 x 10 ½ in.).

RIGHT
Pair, 1989.
Stoneware, 37 x 19 x 8 cm
(14 ½ x 7 ½ x 3 in.).

Schultze, Klaus

German. Born 1927.

Since 1979 Professor of Ceramics at the Academy of Visual Arts in Munich (D). Best known for his brick sculptures, he has been exhibiting throughout Germany and France for over 40 years. Completed many site-specific commissions, especially in Bavaria and in France. Represented by Gallery B15 in Germany (see appendix 2). Collections include: Musée National d'Art Moderne, Paris (F) (see appendix 1); Museum of Applied Art, Hamburg (D). Lives and works in Überlingen (D).

Untitled, 1975.
Brick, 720 x 550 x 210 cm (283 ¾ x 216 ¾ x 83 in.).
Photograph courtesy of Gallery B15, Munich.

Schultze, Klaus
ABOVE
Fountain, 1983–84.
Brick,
500 x 280 x 300 cm
(197 x 110 x 118 in.).
Photograph courtesy of
Gallery B15, Munich.

Head 1, 1988.
Brick, steel,
160 x 200 cm
(63 x 79 in.).
Photograph courtesy of
Gallery B15, Munich.

Shimazu, Esther

American. Born Honolulu, Hawaii (USA), 1957.

Regularly exhibiting since completing MFA at University of Massachusetts/Amhurst (USA) in 1982. Represented by the John Natsoulas Gallery, Davis CA (USA) (see appendix 2). Collections include: Hawaii State Foundation on Culture and Arts, Honolulu (USA); Fresno Art Museum, Fresno, CA (USA). Lives and works in Kailua, Hawaii (USA).

Back Stretch, 1995.
Stoneware,
71 x 38 x 38 cm
(28 x 15 x 15 in.).
Photograph by
David Franzen.

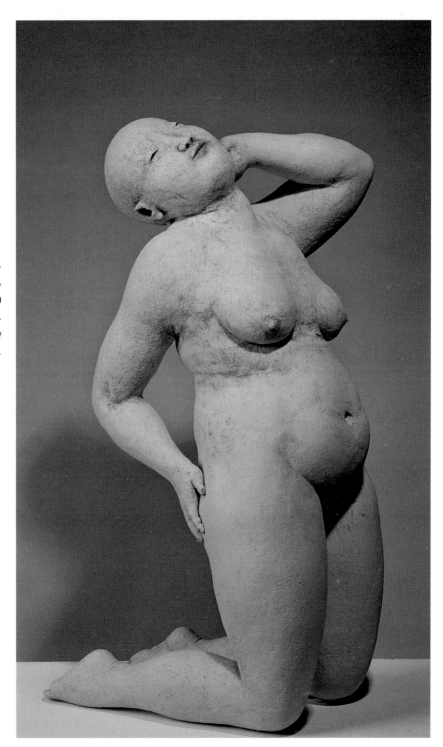

Fish Ups, 1984.
Raku, 23 x 18 x
18 cm (9 x 7 x 7 in.).
Photograph by David
Franzen.

On Hip, 1996.
Stoneware,
33 x 73.5 x 23 cm
(13 x 29 x 9 in.).
Photograph by David
Franzen.

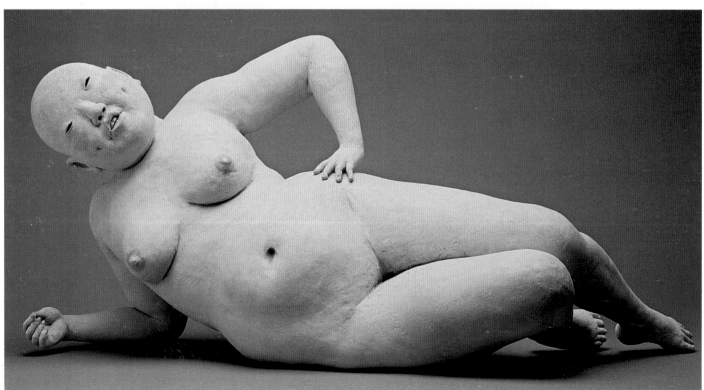

Simon, Laurence

French. Born Paris (F), 1959.

Set up studio in London (GB), having completed MA in Cardiff, Wales (South Glamorgan Institute of Higher Education) in 1981. Collections include: Victoria and Albert Museum, London (GB) (see appendix 1); Shipley Art Gallery, Yorkshire (GB). Lives and works in London (GB).

Seducing the Old Dog, 1998.
Height: 35 cm
(13 ¾ in.).

An Angel Offers Me His Heart, 1996.
Height: 40 cm
(15 ¾ in.).

Musicians, 1997.
Height: 35 cm (13 ¾ in.).

Smolik, Gerda

Austrian. Born Schwarzbach St Veit, Salzburgland (A), 1951.

Works mostly in porcelain although also in raku. Represented by Galerie für Zeitgenössische Keramik, Vienna (A) (see appendix 2). Lives and works in Klagenfurt (A).

Two Women on a Pig, 1998.
Porcelain, height:
40 cm (15 ¾ in.).

Spring Awakening , 1996.
Porcelain, height: 17 cm (6 ¾ in.).

Why Are You So Heavy, 1999. Porcelain, height: 35 cm (13 ¾ in.).

Srivilasa, Vipoo

Thai. Born Bangkok (TH), 1969.

Several exhibitions in Australia since completing MA at University of Tasmania in 1998. Lives and works in St Kilda (AUS).

ABOVE
Mirror, 1994.
Earthenware, coloured
clay, 90 x 60 cm
(35 ½ x 23 ½ in.).

LEFT
Little Mermaids, 1994.
Earthenware, coloured
clay, height (approx.):
15 cm (6 in.).

RIGHT
Sea Lady, 1998.
Earthenware, dry
glaze, slip casting,
45 x 20 cm
(17 ¾ x 8 in.).

RIGHT
Sea Lady, 1998.
Earthenware, dry
glaze, slip casting,
45 x 20 cm
(17 ¾ x 8 in.).

FAR RIGHT
Blue Mermaid, 1997.
Earthenware, barium
glaze, 40 x 30 cm
(15 ¾ x 11 ¾ in.).

BELOW LEFT
Dancing Mermaids,
1994.
Earthenware, coloured
clay, 90 x 60 cm
(35 ½ x 23 ½ in.).

BELOW RIGHT
Mermaid Bottle, 1997.
Earthenware, barium
glaze, 45 x 35 cm
(17 ¾ x 13 ¾ in.).

Stern, Melissa

American. Born Philadelphia, Pennsylvania (USA), 1958.

Works with a mixture of clay, wax, paper and various types of paint. Represented by John Elder Gallery in New York (USA) (see appendix 2). Collections include: Davis Collection, Wesleyan University, Middletown, (USA). Lives and works in New York City (USA).

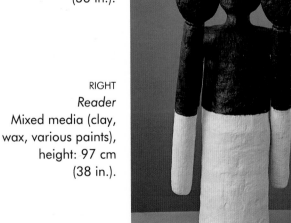

ABOVE
Offering
Mixed media (clay, wax, various paints), height: 91.5 cm (36 in.).

RIGHT
Reader
Mixed media (clay, wax, various paints), height: 97 cm (38 in.).

ABOVE
Back and Forth
Mixed media (clay, wax, various paints), height: 86 cm (34 in.).

LEFT
Heads Up
Mixed media (clay, wax, various paints), height: 109.5 cm (43 in.).

Struktuur 68

Studio for monumental ceramics founded in The Hague in 1968 by Jacques van Gaalen and Henk Trumpie. It has since then completed around 1000 successful commissions in collaboration with more than 200 national and international artists. Through its initial work with Cobra artists like Karel Appel and Lucebert, the studio has developed an amazing range of around 5000 glaze colours. The influence of this work and of the 'Cobra' style is very apparent in much Dutch ceramics.

Wiegman, Diet   Dutch. Born Schiedan (NL), 1944. Completed studies in 1965, in monumental art at the Academy of Visual Arts, Rotterdam, where he has been teaching since 1979. Exhibiting regularly since 1983, mostly in Holland. Collections include: Frans Hals Museum Haarlem (NL), Museum of Art and Industry, Hamburg (D) (see appendix 1). Lives and works in Rotterdam (NL).

Snoeck, Jan   Dutch. Born Rotterdam (NL), 1927. Has exhibited widely in Europe over the last 45 years during which time he has completed a great many commissions for sculptures or reliefs mostly in Holland. From 1947–50 studied sculpture at the Royal academy, The Hague. Worked for a while during 1954 in Ossip Zadkine's studio in Paris. Lives and works in Rotterdam (NL).

Lucebert (pseudonym of Lubertus J. Swaanswijk)   Dutch. Born Amsterdam (NL) 1924. Poet, painter and draughtsman who often collaborated with the Cobra group. One of the protagonists of the 'new Dutch sensibility' of the late 1940s and 1950s. Produced several small ceramic sculptures in Berlin 1980–90. Died Bergen, (NL) 1994.

Wiegman, Diet
David (work in progress), 1989. Fired clay. Photograph by Gunnar Vinje.

Lucebert
Sculpture, 1996.
From a small ceramic
model executed after
the artist died, by
Jacques van Gaalen.
Location: Museum
Kranenburgh, Bergen.
Height: 320 cm
(125.5 in.).
Photograph by
Gunnar Vinje.

Snoeck, Jan
*Woman with Child
and Smoker,* 1993.
Both 190 x 80 x 80 cm
(78 ½ x 31 ½ x 31 ½ in.).
Photograph by
Peer van der Kruis.

Van Bentem, Hans

Dutch. Born The Hague (NL) 1965.

Graduated in Monumental Ceramics at the Royal Academy of Art, The Hague in 1988. Exhibiting regularly since 1990, having also completed several site specific commissions in Holland. Represented by Garth Clark Gallery, New York (USA) (see appendix 2). Lives and works in The Hague (NL).

Guard, 1998.
Glazed ceramic, height: 300 cm (118 in.).
Photograph by Hans van Bentem.

Prosperity, 1997.
Glazed ceramic, height: 250 cm (98 ½ in.).
Photograph by Ernst Moritz.

Freijmuth, Alphons

Dutch. Born Haarlem (NL) 1940.

Since 1974 teacher at Academy for Art and Industry, Enschede (NL). Frequent exhibitions, mostly in Holland and Belgium, since completing studies at Rijksacademie for Visual Arts in Amsterdam (NL) in 1964. Several site-specific commissions in ceramic or bronze in The Netherlands. Lives and works in Amsterdam (NL).

Sun and Square, 1997.
Glazed ceramic, height: 80cm (31½ in.).
Photograph by Ernst Moritz.

Totem 1997
Glazed ceramic, height:
190 cm (75 in.).
Photograph by Ernst Moritz.

Sturm, Robert

German. Born Bad Ester, Saxony (D), 1935.

A pioneer of ceramic sculpture in postwar Germany. Also worked in stone, bronze, steel, aluminium and two-dimensions. From 1964 ceramic became his major medium. Professor of Sculpture at University of Fulda 1971-1994. Member of the International Academy of Ceramics (see p.233). Collections include: Government Collections in Bonn, (D); Bellerive Museum, Zürich (CH) (see appendix 1). Died 1994.

Head, 1992.
Porcelain with engobe and oxide,
height: 40 cm (15 ¾ in.).
Photograph courtesy of Wolf Böwig.

Torso, 1992.
Porcelain with engobe and oxide,
height: 170 cm (67 in.).
Photograph courtesy of Wolf Böwig.

Head, 1988.
Stoneware and raku, with oxides and engobe,
34 x 20 x 24 cm (13 ½ x 8 x 9 ½ in.).
Photograph by Gros, Montabaur.

Takamori, Akio

American. Born Nobeoka, Miyazaki (JAP), 1950.

Professor of Ceramics, University of Washington, Seattle (USA). A major figure in American ceramics for 20 years. Completed MFA at Alfred University, Alfred (USA) in 1978, having previously been a production potter in Japan. Represented by the Garth Clark Gallery in New York (see appendix 2). Work in numerous collections throughout the world (see appendix 1). Lives and works in Seattle (USA).

Figures, 1997.
Whiteware. Height (approx): 35.5 cm (14 in.).
Photograph courtesy of the Garth Clark Gallery.

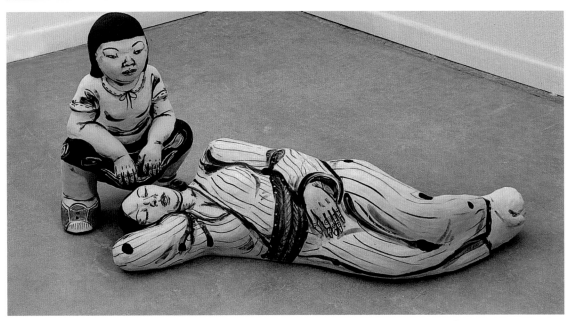

LEFT OF IMAGE
Small Girl, 1997.
Whiteware, height: 34 cm (13 ½ in.).

RIGHT OF IMAGE
Sleeper, 1997.
Whiteware, length: 66 cm (26 in.).
Photograph courtesy of the Garth Clark Gallery.

BELOW
Human, 1987.
Porcelain, 44 x 71 cm
(17 ½ x 28 in.).
Photograph courtesy of
the Garth Clark Gallery.

ABOVE LEFT
Father, Mother and Son, 1988.
Porcelain, 53 x 33 cm (21 x 13 in.).
Photograph courtesy of the Garth Clark Gallery.

ABOVE
Bust of a Woman, 1991.
Porcelain, height: 70 cm (27 ½ in.).
Photograph courtesy of the Garth Clark Gallery.

LEFT
Birth of Buddha, 1995.
Porcelain, 61 x 81 x 28 cm (24 x 32 x 11 in.).
Photograph courtesy of the Garth Clark Gallery.

Triantifillou, Lena

Greek, Born Mytilene, Lesbos (GR) 1951.

Initially studied with her mother, Vanio, a renowned sculptress in Greece. 1991–96 studied Ceramic Art and Technology at the 'Experimental Studio: Art from Clay, Athens'. Exhibits regularly in Greece. Lives and works in Athens (GR).

The Bureaucrat, 1997.
Stoneware and toilet roll,
height: 87cm (34 ½ in.).
Photograph courtesy of Kostas Tarkassis
(Kerameiki Techni Magazine).

The Intellectual, 1995.
Ceramic, wire and egg,
height: 86 cm (34 in.).
Photograph courtesy of Kostas Tarkassis
(Kerameiki Techni Magazine).

Miss Family Bliss, 1997.
Ceramic, mop and ladle,
height: 110 cm (49 ¼ in.).
Photograph courtesy of Kostas Tarkassis
(Kerameiki Techni Magazine).

Tsivin, Vladimir

Russian. Born St Petersburg (formerly Leningrad) (RUS), 1949.

Internationally the best known contemporary Russian ceramic artist. 1972–76 Chief Artist, Bogashevo Experimental Factory, Tomsk, Siberia (RUS). Has designed and made sculptural compositions and architectural ceramics for public buildings in St Petersburg and other Russian cities. Member of the International Academy of Ceramics (see p.233). Represented by Galerie Besson in London (GB) (see appendix 2). Collections include: Museum of Russian Decorative Arts, Moscow (RUS); Museum of Applied Arts, Prague (CZ) (see appendix 1). Lives and works in St Petersburg (RUS).

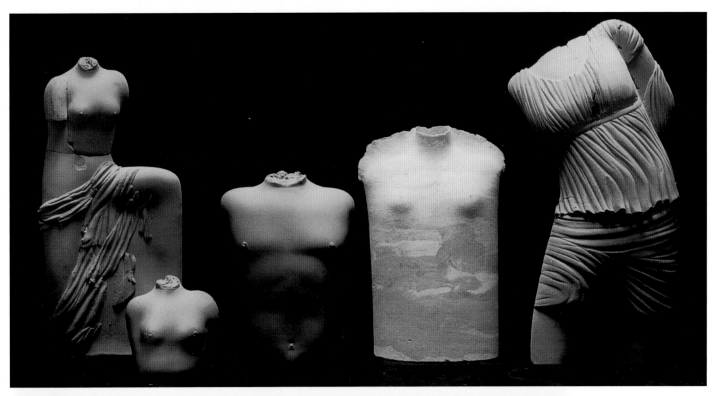

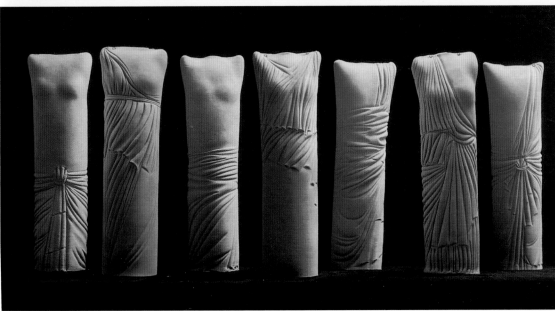

ABOVE
Translations From Greek (From the Antique Cycle), 1980. Terracotta, metallic salts and glaze, height: 44 cm (17 ½ in.).

LEFT
Small Greek Choir (From the Antique Cycle), 1981. Terracotta, metallic salts, engobe, height: 42 cm (16 ½ in.).

RIGHT AND FAR RIGHT
Tsivin, Vladimir
Little Girl, (From Archaic Cycle) 1996, Chamotte, engobe and glaze, height: 33.5 cm (13 ¼ in.).

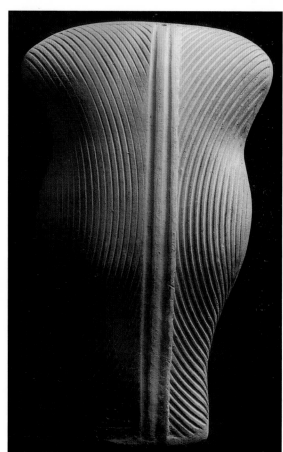

RIGHT
Black Adam (From Archaic Cycle), 1996. Chamotte, engobe, oxide, stone, height: 35.5 cm (14 in.).

FAR RIGHT
Walking Torso (From Egyptian Cycle), 1995. Grogged stoneware, oxide, glaze, height: 35.5 cm (14 in.).

OPPOSITE PAGE
Man and Woman, 1992. White stoneware, porcelain engobe, sandblasted, height: 48.5 cm (19 ⅛ in.). Made in collaboration with Frank Boyden. Photograph by Michael Harvey, courtesy of Galerie Besson.

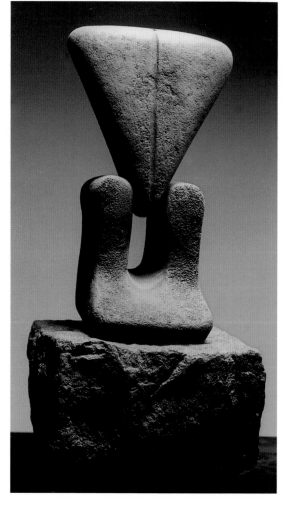

Tsutsumi, Nobuko

Japanese. Born Osaka (JAP), 1958.

Exhibiting frequently in Japan since graduating from Kyoto Municipal Ceramic Laboratory in 1983. Several site-specific sculptures in Japan. Member of the International Academy of Ceramics (see p.233). Collections include: National Museum of Prague (CZ); Shigaraki Ceramic Cultural Park (JAP) (see appendix 1). Lives and works in Osaka (JAP).

OPPOSITE PAGE
Cloudiser, 1999.
320 x 200 x 100 cm
(125 ½ x 79 x 39 ½ in.).

Waterfall.
300 x 100 x 120 cm
(118 x 39 ½ x 47 ¾ in.)

Shi-shin: *Four Gods.*
Various sizes.

Verdcourt, Ann

New Zealander. Born Luton, Bedford (GB), 1934.

Well known in New Zealand, having emigrated there in 1965. Her still life groups of the 1970s preceded those of Gwyn Hanssen-Piggot and Andrew Lord. Her stoneware figures are mostly unglazed, sometimes using engobes, pigment washes or crayon on bisque. Represented by Janneland, Wellington (NZ) (see appendix 2). Collections include: Auckland Museum (NZ) (see appendix 1); Museum of New Zealand Te Papa Tongarewa, Wellington (NZ). Lives and works in Dannevirke (NZ).

Knee, 1998.
Black body, manganese, copper,
height: 70 cm (27 ½ in.).

Ceremonial Elbow, 1997.
Stoneware, height: 50 cm (20 in.).

Mermaids, 1998.
Black stoneware body, manganese wash, width: 40–48 cm (15 ¾ –19 in.).

I've Only Met Richard At Parties, 1998.
Stoneware, height (largest): approx. life-size.

Wind (from series: Something About Columbus), 1992. Stoneware, width: 19 cm (7 ½ in.).

Wind No. 2 (from series: Something About Columbus), 1992. Stoneware, width: 19 cm (7 ½ in.).

Cannibals (from series: Something About Columbus), 1992. Stoneware.

Sailors (from series: Something About Columbus), 1992. Stoneware, width: 55 cm (22 in.).

Vermeersch, José

Belgian. Born Bissegem, Flanders (B), 1922.

A pioneer who turned to ceramics when he was almost 50 years old. He had previously worked as a painter and sculptor, having studied at the Antwerp Academy of Fine Art (B) before the War and again in 1944. Although very much a loner when figuration was not popular, has nevertheless had a considerable influence on modern Flemish ceramics. His ceramic pieces were fired using a 'field kiln' which was a modification of the old pit-firing technique. Collections include: Frans Hals Museum, Haarlem (NL) (see appendix 1); The Openair Sculpture Museum, Middleheim (B). Died Lendele (B), 1997.

Child on a Dog, 1988
Pit-fired terracotta (*see above*), height: 72 cm (28 ¼ in.)

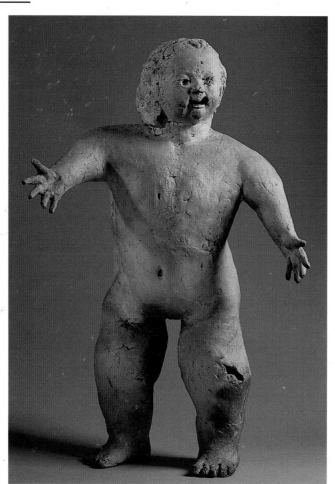

RIGHT
Pascal II, 1969.
Height: 73 cm
(28 ¾ in.).

FAR RIGHT
Pascal III, 1974.
Height: 70 cm
(27 ½ in.).

BELOW
Kennel, 1977–78.
Height: various sizes
up to 145 cm (57 in.).

Viková, Jindra

Czech. Born Prague (CZ), 1946.

Internationally probably the best known Czech ceramic artist, having won many prestigious awards and regularly exhibiting throughout the world. Member of the International Academy of Ceramics (see p.233). Collections include: National Gallery, Prague (CZ), International Ceramic Museum, Kecskemét (H) (see appendix 1). Lives and works in Bernice near Prague (CZ).

Whispering, 1998.
Stoneware, 44.5 x 52 x 24 cm (17.5 x 20.5 x 9.5 in.).
Photograph courtesy of Pavel Baňka.

LEFT
Small Surprising, 1974.
Maiolica, height: 30 cm (11 ¾ in.).
Photograph courtesy of Pauel Baňka.

BELOW
Hovor Talk, 1993.
Stoneware, height: 32 x 22 cm (12 ½ x 8 ¾ in.).
Photograph courtesy of Pauel Baňka.

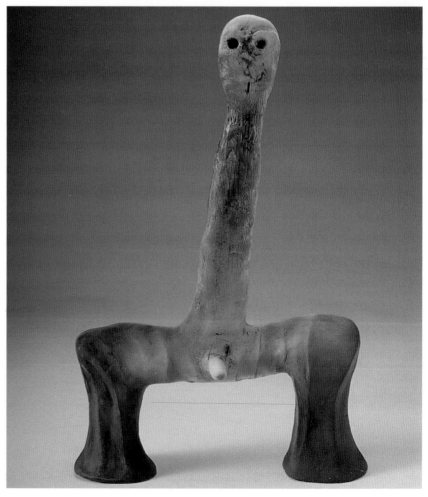

ABOVE
Totem of Family Balance, 1991.
Porcelain, height: 50 cm (20 in.).
Photograph courtesy of Pauel Baňka.

RIGHT
Totem of Happiness, 1995.
Porcelain, height: 48 cm (19 in.).
Photograph courtesy of Pauel Baňka.

Unknown Man, 1983.
Porcelain, height: 45 cm (17 ¾ in.).
Photograph courtesy of Pavel Baňka.

Walker, George

British. Date and place of birth withheld but studied painting at Harrow School of Art (now University of Westminster), London (GB), 1950.

Turned to ceramics in 1972. Represented by Maureen Michaelson in London (GB) (see appendix 2). Collections: Ulster Museum, Northern Ireland (GB) (see appendix 1); University of Texas, El Paso (USA). Lives and works in London (GB).

'The Lamia of Rodin'
(Camille Clauel), 1993.
Height: 47 cm (18 ½ in.).

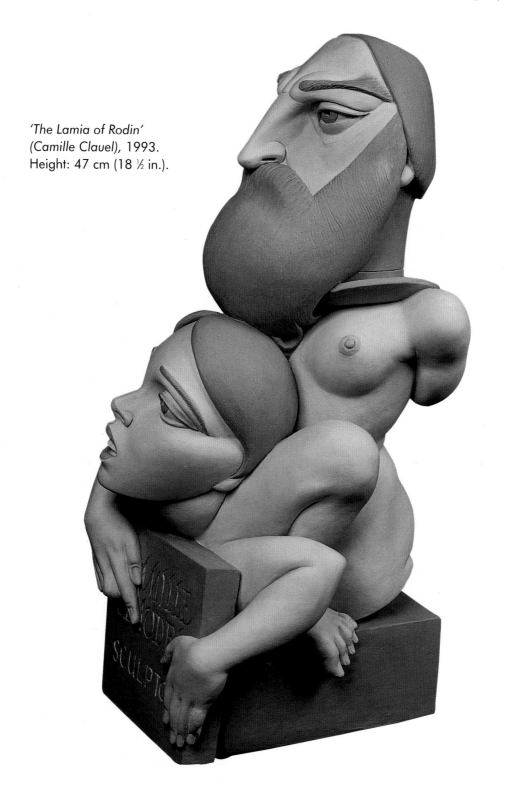

Williams, Gary

Canadian. Born Calgary (CAN), 1956.

Since 1990, instructor at Alberta College of Art, Calgary (CAN). Collections include: Alberta Art Foundation, Edmonton (CAN); Burlington Cultural Centre, Burlington, Ontario (CAN). Lives and works in Calgary (CAN).

David. View of Gary Walker's installation
at the Gardiner Museum, Toronto 1998.
Porcelain figures on steel tables, height (figures): 89 cm (35 in.).

Wood, Beatrice

American. Born San Francisco, California (USA), 1893.

Highly celebrated figure in American ceramics. Remarkable life including relationship with Marcel Duchamp and thus involvement in the New York Dada movement. Began making ceramics at the age of 40. Figurative work only a part of her output. Also produced a great many vessels. Refers to her figures as 'sophisticated primitives'. Represented by Frank Lloyd Gallery in Los Angeles and Garth Clark in New York (USA) (see appendix 2). Work in numerous American collections (see appendix 1). Died Oji, CAL (USA), 1998.

Career Women, 1990.
Earthenware.
49 x 32 x 25.5 cm
(19 ½ x 12 ½ x 10 in.).
Photograph by Anthony
Cunha, courtesy of Frank
Lloyd Gallery, L. A.

RIGHT
The Artist, 1990.
Glazed Earthenware,
height: 41 cm (16 in.).
Photograph by Anthony
Cunha, courtesy of Frank
Lloyd Gallery, L. A.

FAR RIGHT
Priscilla, 1996.
Earthenware,
29.5 x 25.5 cm
(11 ½ x 10 in.).
Photograph by Anthony
Cunha, courtesy of Frank
Lloyd Gallery, L. A.

The Man Who Thought He Had Arrived, 1993.
Earthenware, height: 50 cm (20 in.).
Photograph by Anthony Cunha, courtesy of Frank Lloyd Gallery, L. A.

Woodward, John

American. Born Michigan (USA).

Regularly exhibiting in America over the last 20 years. Represented by Nancy Margolis in New York (see appendix 2). Collection: Detroit Institute of Arts, Detroit, Michigan (USA) (see appendix 1). Lives and works in Detroit, Michigan (USA).

Brazos River, 2000.
Painted ceramic. 81 x 50 x 46 cm
(32 x 20 x 18 in.).

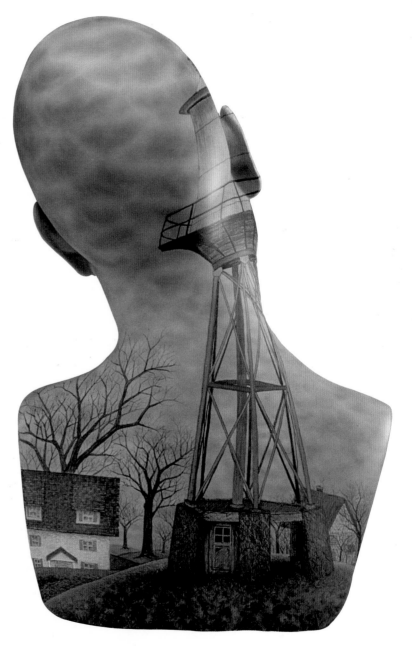

1 Water Tower, 1996.
Painted ceramic. 74 x 41 x 46 cm
(29 x 16 x 18 in.).

Yatom, Varda

Israeli. Born Holon (ISR), 1946.

A highly regarded artist in Israel who exhibits widely throughout the world. Collections include: The International Museum of Ceramic Art at Alfred, New York (USA); Hetjens Museum, Düsseldorf (D) (see appendix 1). Lives and works in Kibbutz Sasa (ISR).

Figure, 1986.
Earthenware, plastic,
100 x 40 x 55 cm
(39 ½ x 15 ¾ x 22 in.).

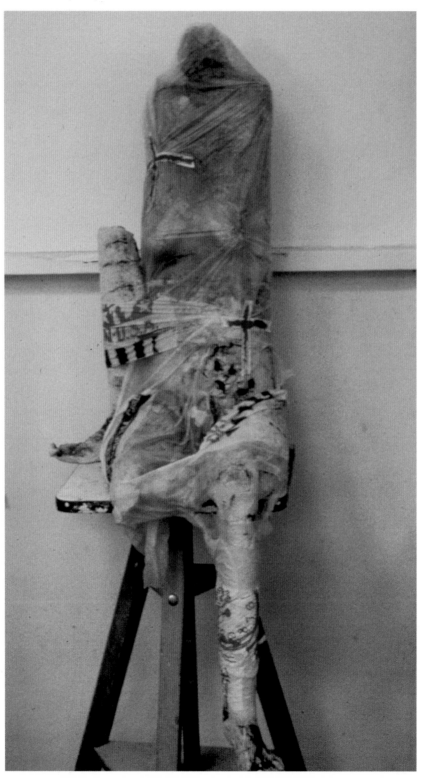

ABOVE
*Installation: Human
Beings,* 1987.
Plastic, unfired clay,
150–80 x 40 cm
(60–71 x 15 ¾ in.).

RIGHT
Embryos (part of an
installation), 1987.
Stoneware,
50 x 120 x 40 cm
(20 x 47 ¾ x 15 ¾ in.).

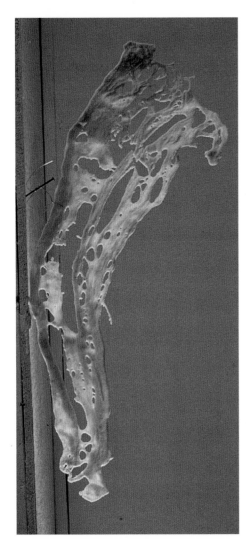

ABOVE
*Grinding Stones No.2
(Installation)*, 1990.
Earthenware, stone, textile,
wire, 67–70 x 50 x 40 cm
(26–27 ½ x 20 x 15 ¾ in.).

LEFT
Figure, 1987.
Porcelain. 40 x 420 x 2 cm
(15 ¾ x 195 ½ x ¾ in.).

ABOVE
Laucon, 1992.
Earthenware, 80 x 80 x 40 cm (31 ½ x 31 ½ x 15 ¾ in.).

RIGHT
Standing Or Hanging?, 1988.
Porcelain, white clay, white textile, height: 250 cm (98 ½ in.).

Youngblood, Daisy

American. Born Asheville, North Carolina (USA), 1945.

Represented by the Mckee Gallery in New York (see appendix 2). Collections: Mint Museum, North Carolina (USA); Newark Museum, New Jersey, (USA) (see appendix 1). Lives and works in New Mexico (USA).

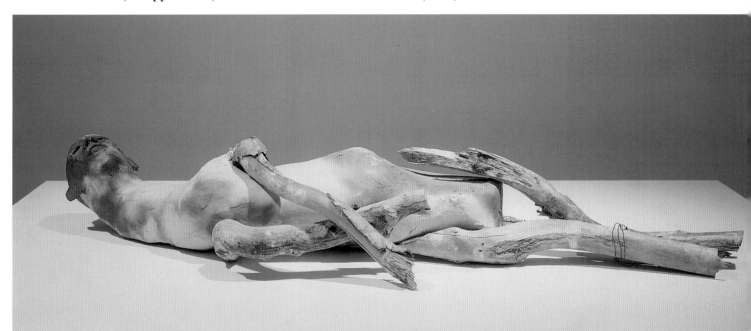

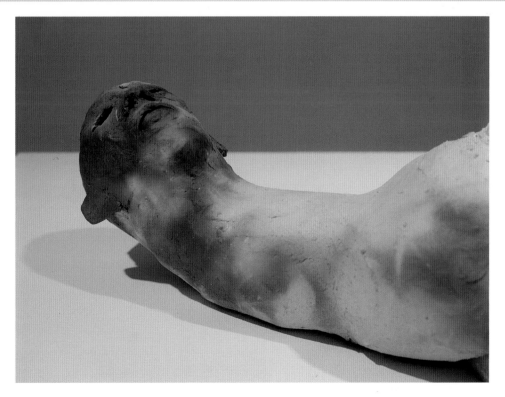

TOP AND BOTTOM (DETAIL)
Tied Goat, 1983.
Clay and wood, 15 x 12 ¼ x 28 cm (6 x 31 ½ x 11 in.).
Photograph courtesy of Franklin Parrasch Gallery, New York.

RIGHT
Wiggling, 1981.
Unglazed, fired clay,
72.5 x 21.5 x 30 cm
(28 ½ x 8 ½ x 11 ¾ in.).
Photograph courtesy of
McKee Gallery, New York.

FAR RIGHT
Watching Girl, 1983.
Low-fired clay, sticks
and hair,
43 x 38 x 39 cm
(17 x 15 x 15 ½ in.).
Photograph courtesy of
McKee Gallery, New York.

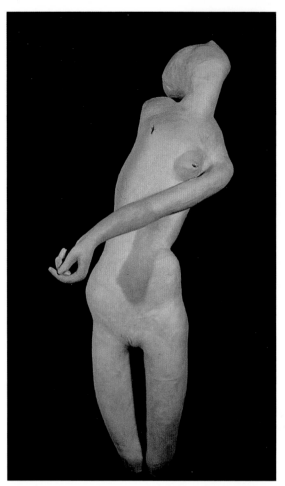

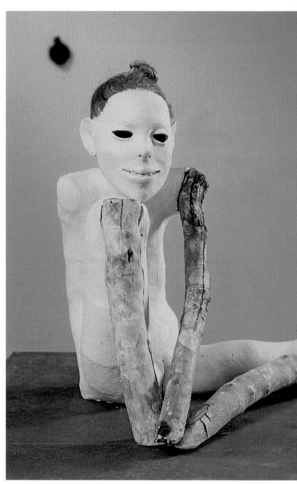

RIGHT
Keeping Still, 1991.
Low-fired clay,
24 x 10 x 10 ½ in.
(61 x 25.5 x 27 cm).
Photograph courtesy of
McKee Gallery, New York.

FAR RIGHT
Roberta, 1987.
Low-fired clay,
12.5 x 12.5 x 11.5 cm
(5 x 5 x 4 ½ in.).
Photograph courtesy of
McKee Gallery, New York.

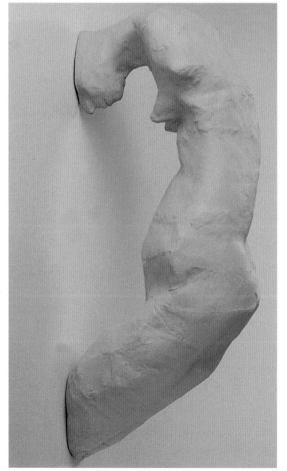

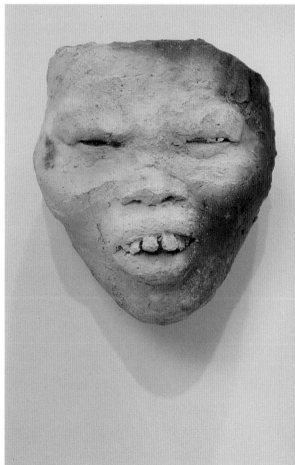

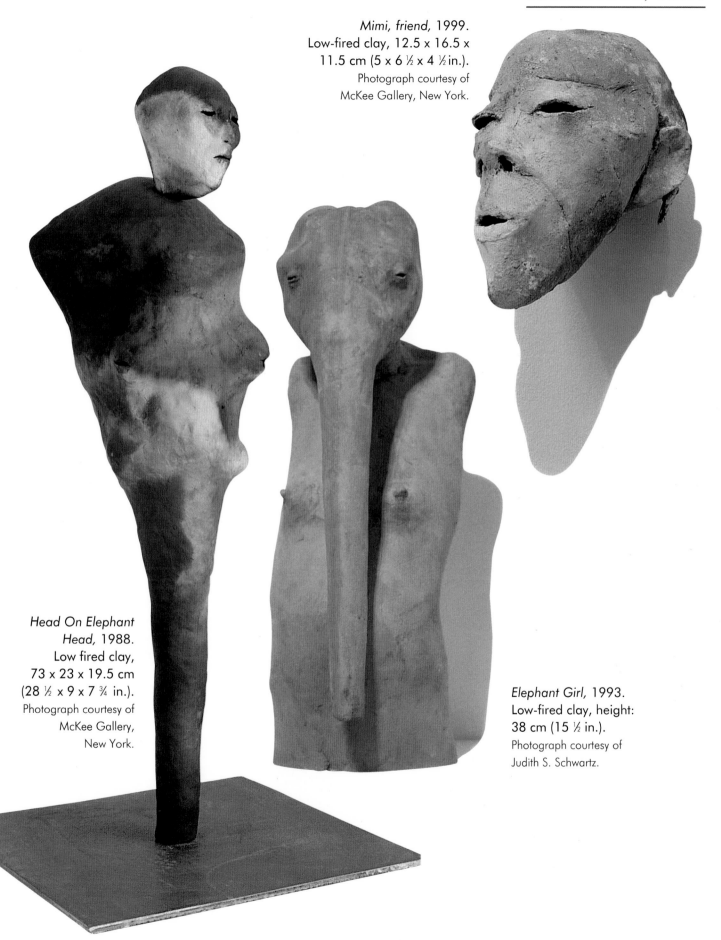

Mimi, friend, 1999.
Low-fired clay, 12.5 x 16.5 x
11.5 cm (5 x 6 ½ x 4 ½ in.).
Photograph courtesy of
McKee Gallery, New York.

*Head On Elephant
Head,* 1988.
Low fired clay,
73 x 23 x 19.5 cm
(28 ½ x 9 x 7 ¾ in.).
Photograph courtesy of
McKee Gallery,
New York.

Elephant Girl, 1993.
Low-fired clay, height:
38 cm (15 ½ in.).
Photograph courtesy of
Judith S. Schwartz.

Zamorska, Anna-Malicka

Polish. Born Lubien, Nr Lvov (PL), 1942.

At the forefront of contemporary Polish ceramic art. Exhibits widely in Europe. Member of the International Academy of Ceramics (see p.233). Represented by Gallery Opera, Warsaw (PL). Collections include: International Ceramic Studio, Kecskemét (H); The National Museum, Wroclaw (PL) (see appendix 1). Lives and works in Wroclaw (PL).

I'm Happy, 1992.
Slipcast porcelain, height: 200 cm (78 ¾ in.).

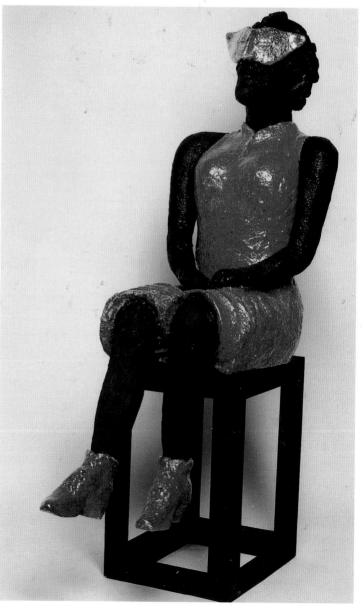

ABOVE
Macho, 1995. Height: 102 cm (40 ¼ in.).

ABOVE RIGHT
Lion, 1998.
Height: 55 cm (22 in.).

RIGHT
Anna, 1998.
Height: 80 cm (31 ½ in.).

Some Collections Where Artists Work Can Be Seen

AUSTRALIA

National Museum of Victoria, Melbourne:
Ruth and Alan Barrett-Danes, Glenys Barton, Anthony Bennett, Carmen Dionyse, Maria Kuczynska, Jindra Viková.

Perth Art Gallery of Western Australia:
Ruth and Alan Barrett-Danes, Anthony Bennett, Carmen Dionyse, Gudrun Klix.

Power House Museum, Sydney:
Carmen Dionyse, Fiona Fell, Alan Peascod, Jindra Viková.

CANADA

Canadian Clay and Glass Museum, Waterloo, Ontario:
Michel Flynn, Greg Payce, Vladimir Tsivin.

The George R. Gardiner Museum of Ceramic Art, Toronto:
Viola Frey, Georges Jeanclos, Takio Akomori.

CZECH REPUBLIC

Agency for Czech Design, Cesky-Krumlov:
Michael Flynn, Miroslav Parel, Jindra Viková.

Museum of Applied Arts, Prague:
Gundi Dietz, Michael Flynn, Sandor Kecseméti, Hana Purkrábková, Vladimir Tsivin, Jindra Viková.

Museum of International Ceramics, Bechyne:
Carmen Dionyse, Nica Haug, Vladimir Tsivin.

National Gallery, Prague:
Gérard Bignolais, Carmen Dionyse, Nobuko Tsutsumi, Jindra Viková.

DENMARK

Grimmerhus Museum, Middlefart:
Michael Flynn, Nina Hole.

Museum of Art and Industry, Copenhagen:
Nina Hole.

FRANCE

Musée National d'Art Moderne, Centre Georges Pompidou, Paris:
Daphné Corregan, Georges Jeanclos, Klaus Schultze.

Musée National de Ceramique, Sèvres:
Christie Brown, Roger Capron, Viola frey.

GERMANY

Baden-Württembergisches Landesmuseum, Stuttgart:
Daphné Corregan, Jill Crowley, Carmen Dionyse, Lothar Fischer, Michael Flynn, Nica Haug, Theresia Hebenstreit, Gertraud Möhwald, Jindra Viková.

Egner Collection, Frechen:
Ruth and Alan Barrett-Danes, Christie Brown, Carmen Dionyse, Michael Flynn, Maria Geszler, Theresia Hebenstreit, Maria Kuczynska, Sally Macdonnell, Gisela Schmidt-Reuther, Imre Schrammel, Robert Sturm, Jindra Viková.

Hetjens Museum, Düsseldorf:
Carmen Dionyse, Lothar Fischer, Gisela Schmidt-Reuther, Imre Schrammel, Varda Yatom.

Institut für Künstlerische Keramik und Glas, Höhr-Grenzhausen:
Carmen Dionyse, Michael Flynn, Maria Geszler, Sándor Kecseméti, Gudrun Klix, Maria Kuczynska, Gertraud Möhwald, Imre Schrammel, Robert Sturm.

Keramikmuseum Westerwald, Höhr-Grenzhausen:
Roger Capron, Jill Crowley, Carmen Dionyse, Michael Flynn, Maria Geszler, Sándor Kecseméti, Maria Kuczynska, Gertraud Möhwald, Gisela Schmidt-Reuthers, Robert Sturm.

Keramion, Frechen:
Carmen Dionyse, Michael Flynn, Maria Kuczynska, Gertraud Möhwald, Jindra Viková.

Sammlung der Kreissparkasse Westerwald, Montabauer:
Michael Flynn, Maria Geszler, Sándor Kecseméti, Gudrun Klix, Imre Schrammel.

GREAT BRITAIN

Aberystwyth Art Centre (University of Wales), Aberystwyth:
Michael Flynn, Nina Hole, Vladimir Tsivin, Anna Malicka Zamorska.

Birmingham Museum and Art Gallery, Birmingham:
Ruth and Alan Barrett-Danes, Glenys Barton.

Crafts Council of Great Britain, London:
Glenys Barton, Sandy Brown, Neil Brownsword, Jill Crowley, Clare Curneen, Stephen Dixon, Philip Eglin, Michael Flynn, Geoffrey Fuller, Mo Jupp.

Fitzwilliam Museum, Cambridge:
Philip Eglin, Michael Flynn.

Leicester Museum and Art Gallery, Leicester:
Glenys Barton, Geoffrey Fuller.

National Museum of Wales, Cardiff:
Ruth and Alan Barrett-Danes, Michael Flynn, Achille Pauwels.

Royal Museum of Scotland, Edinburgh:
Glenys Barton, Christie Brown, Craig Mitchell.

Sculpture at Goodwood, Goodwood, East Sussex:
Alan Jones, Sean Henry.

Shipley Art Gallery, Gateshead:
Stephen Dixon, Michael Flynn, Laurance Simon.

Ulster Museum, Belfast, N. Ireland:
Ruth and Alan Barrett-Danes, Anthony Bennett, Clare Curneen, Christy Keeney, Stephen Dixon, George Walker.

Victoria and Albert Museum, London:
Rudi Autio, Glenys Barton, Christie Brown, Sandy Brown, Philip Eglin, Michael Flynn, Geoffrey Fuller, Mo Jupp, Howard Kottler, Imre Schrammel, Laurance Simon, Akio Takamori, Beatrice Wood.

HUNGARY

International Ceramic Museum, Kecskemét:
Laszlo Fekete, Michael Flynn, Geörgy Fusz, Maria Geszler, Nina Hole, Sergei Isupov, Sándor Kecseméti, Maria Kuczynska, Jolante Kvasyte, Miroslav Paral, Imre Schrammel, Robert Sturm, Vladimir Tsivin, Jindra Viková, Anna-Malicka Zamorska.

Janos Pannonius Museum, Pecs:
Maria Geszler, Geörgy Fusz, Sándor Kecseméti, Imre Schrammel.

Museum of Applied Arts, Budapest:
Laszlo Feketi, Maria Geszler, Geörgy Fusz, Sándor Kecseméti, Imre Schrammel.

ISRAEL

University of Beer Sheva:
Michael Flynn, Marion Held, Vladimir Tsivin, Varda Yatom.

ITALY

International Ceramic Museum, Faenza:
Roger Capron, Carmen Dionyse, Maria Kuczynska, Imre Schrammel, Vladimir Tsivin, Jindra Viková.

JAPAN

Shigaraki Ceramic Cultural Park (Museum of Contemporary Ceramic Art):
Rudi Autio, Tony Bennett, Toby Buonagurio, Jill Crowley, Carmen Dionyse, Viola Frey, Sándor Kecskeméti, Maria Kuczynska, Akio Takamori, Nobuko Tsutsumi.

NETHERLANDS

Boymans-Van Beuningen Museum Rotterdam:
Glenys Barton, Carmen Dionyse, Jan Snoeck, Diet Wiegman.

Frans Hals Museum, Haarlem:
Diet Wiegman, José Vermeersch.

Het Kruithuis, s-Hertogenbosch:
Michael Flynn, Maria Kuczynska, Sándor Kecskeméti, Akio Takomori.

Stedelijk Museum, Amsterdam:
Robert Arneson, Mark Burns, Philip Eglin, Alphons Freijmuth, Jan Snoeck.

NEW ZEALAND

Auckland Museum, Auckland:
Tony Bennett, Ann Verdcourt.

NORWAY

Museum of Art and Industry, Oslo:
Rudi Autio, Diet Wiegman.

Museum of Art and Industry, Trondheim:
Michael Flynn, Diet Wiegman.

POLAND

Museum of Porcelain, Walbrzych:
Michael Flynn, Maria Kuczynska, Kazimierz Kalkowski, Jolante Kvasyte, Vladimir Tsivin, Jindra Viková, Anna Malicka Zamorska.

The National Museum of Art, Wroclaw:
Michael Flynn, Maria Kuczynska, Kazimierz Kalkowski, Jolante Kvasyte, Vladimir Tsivin, Anna Malicka Zamorska.

SWITZERLAND

Bellerive Museum, Zürich:
Carmen Dionyse, Maria Kuczynska, Robert Sturm.

International Academy of Ceramics
Musée Ariana, 10 Avenue de la Paix, CH 1202, Geneva
Tel: (4122) 418 5476
Fax: (4122) 418 5451

Geneva based association of ceramic artists, historians, critics, colleges and galleries committed to the support and furtherance of ceramic art throughout the world. Membership, which is for life, is through election which takes place every two years.

Musée Ariana, Geneva:
Roger Capron, Carmen Dionyse, Laszlo Fekete, Michael Flynn, Maria Geszler, Sándor Kecskeméti, Maria Kuczynska, Gertraud Möhwald, Gisela Schmidt-Reuther, Imre Schrammel, Vladimir Tsivin, Jindra Viková, Anna Malicka Zamorska.

Museum of History and Porcelains, Château de Nyon, Nyon:
Michael Flynn, Jindra Viková.

Nievergelt Collection, Ramsen:
Michael Flynn, Sándor Kecskeméti.

TAIWAN

Taipei Fine Arts Museum:
Fiona Fell, Gisela schmidt-Reuther.

USA

The International Museum of Ceramic Art at Alfred, Alfred, NY:
Doug Jeck, Howard Kottler, Varda Yatom.

Art Institute of Chicago, Chicago, IL:
Robert Arneson, Jack Earl, Mary Frank, Michelle Oka Doner.

American Craft Museum, New York, NY:
Robert Arneson, Rudi Autio, Toby Buonagurio, Stephen de Staebler, Jack Earl, Viola Frey, Arthur Gonzalez, Howard Kottler, Judy Moonellis, Michelle Oka Doner, Beatrice Wood.

Baltimore Museum of Art, MD:
Michael Flynn, Mary Frank.

Boston Museum of Fine Art, Boston, MA:
Robert Arneson, Rudi Autio, Howard Kottler, Wayne Fischer, Beatrice Wood.

Cooper Hewitt Museum, New York, NY:
Gundi Dietz, Howard Kottler, Beatrice Wood.

Detroit Institute of Arts, Detroit, MI:
Rudi Autio, Viola Frey, Howard Kottler, Michelle Oka Doner, John Woodward, Beatrice Wood.

Everson Museum of Art, Syracuse, NY:
Rudi Autio, Toby Buonagurio, Mark Burns, Stephen de Staebler, Jack Earl, Mary Frank, Viola Frey, Arthur Gonzalez, Howard Kottler, Michael Lucero, Judy Moonellis, Justin Novak, Beatrice Wood.

Jewish Museum, New York, NY:
Mary Frank, Georges Jeanclos.

Kansas City Art Institute, Kansas, MO:
Howard Kottler, Akio Takamori.

The Kolher Art Centre, Sheboygan, WI:
Many artists.

Los Angeles County Museum, CA:
Rudi Autio, Viola Frey, Sergei Isupov, Doug Jeck, Howard Kottler, Akio Takamori, Beatrice Wood.

Metropolitan Museum of Art, New York:
Robert Arneson, Rudi Autio, Mary Frank, Viola Frey, Michael Lucero, Beatrice Wood.

Mint Museum, Charlotte, NC:
Toby Buonagurio, Stephen de Staebler, Stephen Dixon, Philip Eglin, Michael Flynn, Arthur Gonzalez, Sergei Isupov, Judy Moonellis, Justin Novak, Daisy Youngbood.

New Jersey State Museum, Trenton, NJ:
Mary Frank, Marion Held.

Newark Museum, Newark, NJ:
Mary Frank, Marion Held, Daisy Youngblood.

Racine Museum, Racine, WI:
Jack Earl, Stephen Dixon, Sergei Isupov, Akio Takamori.

Renwick Gallery, Smithsonian Institution, Washington DC:
Rudi Autio, Jack Earl, Mary Frank, Howard Kottler, Judy Moonellis.

Virginia Museum of Fine Arts, Richmond, VI:
Michael Flynn, Mary Frank, Michelle Oka Doner.

Whitney Museum of American Art, New York, NY:
Robert Arneson, Mary Frank, Viola Frey, Howard Kottler.

Please note: Ceramic collections mentioned in the book have only been listed in Appendix 1 if they show work belonging to two or more of the artists included in the book (or if they are particularly important), due to lack of space.

233

Galleries Representing Artists

Barrett Marsden Gallery
17–18 Great Sutton Street,
London EC1V ODN (GB).
Tel 0207 336 6391
Fax 0207 336 6391
email: info@bmgallery.co.uk

Philip Eglin. Also shows work of Jill Crowley, Stephen Dixon, Mo Jupp.

Berkeley Square Gallery
23a Bruton Street,
London W1X 8JJ (GB).
Tel 020 7493 7939
Fax 020 7493 7798
www.berkeley-square-gallery.co.uk
email: art@berkeley-square-gallery.co.uk

Sean Henry.

D C Moore Gallery
724 Fifth Avenue, New York
NY 10019 (USA).
Tel 212 247 2111
Fax 212 247 2119. www.artnet.com
email: dcmooregal@earthlink.net

Mary Frank.

Ferrin Gallery
163 Teatown Road, Croton on
Hudson, NY 10520, (USA).
Tel 914 271 9362
www.ferringallery.com

Sergei Isupov, Mark Burns.

Flowers East,
199-205 Richmond Road,
London E8 3NJ (GB).
Tel 0208 985 3333
Fax 0208 985 0067.
www.flowerseast.com
email: gallery@flowerseast.com

Glenys Barton.

Frank Lloyd Gallery
2525 Michigan Ave; B5B-Santa
Monica-CA 90404 (USA).
Tel 310 264 3866
Fax 310 264 3868
www.franklloyd.com
email: flloydgall@aol.com

Mark Burns, Viola Frey, Beatrice Wood.

Franklin Parrasch Gallery, Inc.
20 West 57th Street, New York
NY10018 (USA).
Tel 212 246 5380
Fax 212 246 5391
www.franklinparrasch.com
email: franklin@franklinparrasch.com

Stephen de Staebler, Michael Flynn.

Galerie Besson
15 Royal Arcade, 28 Old Bond Street,
London W1X 3HD (GB).
Tel 0207 491 1706
Fax 0207 495 3203
www.galeriebesson.co.uk
email: enquiries@galeriebesson.co.uk

Vladimir Tsivin. Also stocks work by Mo Jupp.

Galerie für Zeitgenossische Keramik, Vienna.
Nussdorfer Strasse, 52
Vienna 1060 (A).
Tel 01 317 3396

Gerda Smolik.

Gallery Opera
ul.Freta 14, Warsaw (PL).
Tel 022 843 88 81

Anna Malicka-Zamorska.

Garth Clark Gallery
24 West 57th Street, New York
NY 10019-3918 (USA).
Tel 212 246 2205.
Fax 212 489 5168. www.garthclark.com
email: info@garthclark.com

Anthony Bennett, Philip Eglin, Laszlo Fekete, Lucio Fontana, Hans van Bentem, Doug Jeck, Akio Takamori, , Beatrice Wood.

George Adams Gallery
41 West 57th Street,
New York 10019 (USA).
Tel 212 644 5665.
Fax 212 644 5666.
www.artnet.com/gadams.html

Robert Arneson.

Helen Drutt Gallery
1721 Walnut Street,
Philadelphia, PA 19103 (USA).
Tel 215 735 1625
Fax 215 732 1382
www.helendrutt.com

Mark Burns.

Janneland Wellington
Furnace Lane, Wellington (NZ).
Tel 04 384 2912

Ann Verdcourt.

John Elder Gallery
529 West 20th street, 7th floor, New
York NY10011 (USA).
Tel 212 462 2600
Fax 212 462 2510
www.johnelder.com
email: mail@johnelder.com

Arthur Gonzalez, Judy Moonellis, Melissa Stern.

John Natsoulas Gallery
521 First street, Davis, CA 95616 (USA).
Tel 530 756 3938
Fax 530 756 3961
email: art@natsoulas.com

Arthur Gonzalez, Sean Henry.

Maureen Michaelson
27 Daleham Gardens, Hampstead,
London NW3 5BY (GB).
Tel 0207 435 0510
Fax 0207 681 0447
email: maureenmichaelson@mac.com

Tracey Heyes, George Walker.

McKee Gallery
745 Fifth Avenue, New York,
NY 10151 (USA).
Tel 212 688 5951
Fax 212 752 5638.
www.mckeegallery.com
email: info@mckeegallery.com

Daisy Youngblood.

Nancy Hoffman Gallery
429 West Broadway New York,
NY 10012 (USA).
Tel 212 966 6676
Fax 212 334 5078.

Viola Frey.

Nancy Margolis Gallery,
560 Broadway, Suite 302.
New York, NY 10012 (USA).
Tel 212 343 95232.
Fax 212 343 9524.

Stephen Dixon, Jack Earl, Greg Payce, John Woodward.

Peter's Barn
South Ambersham, Nr Midhurst,
West Sussex, GU29 OBX (GB).
Tel 01798 861388.

Mo Jupp.

Perimeter Gallery
210 W. Superior Street,
Chicago, IL 60610 (USA).
Tel 312 266 9473
Fax 312 266 7984
www.perimetergallery.com

Christie Brown, Jack Earl.

Prime Gallery
52 McCall street, Toronto,
Ontario (CAN).
Tel 416 593 5750.

Greg Payce.

Salander-O'Reilly Galleries, LLC
20 E79 street, New York, NY 10021
(USA).
Tel 212 879-6606.
Fax 212 744-0655. www.salander.com

Elie Nadelman.

THE WORK OF MOST BRITISH ARTISTS CAN USUALLY BE SEEN AT:

The Crafts Council Gallery Shop
44a Pentonville Road, London N1 9BY
(GB).
Tel 020 7806 2559
Fax 020 7837 6891
www.craftscouncil.org.uk
email: trading@craftscouncil.org.uk

The Crafts Council Shop at the V&A
Victoria and Albert Museum,
London SW7 2RL (GB).
Tel 020 7589 5070
Fax 020 7581 2128
www.craftscouncil.org.uk
email: trading@craftscouncil.org.uk

Contemporary Applied Arts
2 Percy street, London W1T 1DD (GB).
Tel 0207 436 2344
Fax 0207 436 2446
www.caa.org.uk

MOST GERMAN CERAMIC ARTISTS ARE SHOWN BY:

Galerie B15
Baaderstr. 15,
80469 Munich.
Tel 089 202 10 10
Fax 089 642 14 45
email: b15gallery-wunderle@t-online.de

Galerie Marianne Heller
Friedrich-Ebert-Anlage 2, Am
Stadtgarten, D-69117 Heidleberg.
Tel 0 62 21/61 90 90
Fax 0 62 21/61 90 95
www.galerie-heller.de